# How To
# Build A Chopper

Timothy Remus

Published by:
Wolfgang Publications Inc.
1310 Sunny Slope Lane
Stillwater, MN 55082
http://www.wolfgangpublications.com

First published in 2001 by Wolfgang Publications Inc., 1310 Sunny Slope Lane, Stillwater MN 55082

ISBN number: 1-929133-06-5

Printed and bound in the USA

# How To
# Build A Chopper

# Acknowledgements

Never finish today what you can put off until tomorrow. Which means that as always I've put off writing my "thank you note" until the very last. Until the hour before the book ships to the printer.

Let me start by expressing my gratitude to the shops and individual mechanics who let me hang around and ask endless questions. The list starts with Arlen and Cory Ness. Father and son and crew always make me welcome and provide another reason to escape Minnesota in January. Closer to home is the shop of Neil Ryan from American Thunder. Neil finds a way to match my needs with his projects, then turns me over to Ken and Troy who've learned the trick of stopping in middle of installing a wheel or fender so I can snap the shutter and avoid blurry photos. Last though not least is Donnie Smith and crew. I'm indebted to Donnie for letting me in the door, and to Rob and to Don for helping me create the sequences seen a little farther along in the book.

After all these years I've gotten to know good people working in the art and advertising departments at all the big aftermarket companies. From Kip at CCI to Tracy at Biker's Choice and Buck at Rivera. I issue a collective thanks to one and all for sending good images and doing it on short notice.

I see these books as a means of communication between the professional bike builders and all the people who strive to build bikes of professional quality. Interviews are a very good way to do exactly that, though it requires time and patience from the individuals being interviewed. Thus I have to express my gratitude to Barry Cooney, Pat Kennedy, Donnie Smith (again), Tom Johnson from S&S and John Ventriglia from Primo Belt Drives. Collectively they possess well over a hundred years worth of experience building and riding choppers.

For layout and design I rely on an old friend, Mike Urseth. For patience and support (both moral and immoral) I close with a thanks to my lovely and talented wife, Mary Lanz.

# Introduction

The wheels of fashion go round and round and we find ourselves embracing a motorcycle style made popular more than thirty years ago. Many of those choppers were pretty crude by today's standards, with little real engineering, drum brakes and questionable handling. In spite of all their shortcomings choppers were very cool, extremely popular and uniquely American.

They were also the first scratch-built bikes. With a catalog from Jammer's or AEE the intrepid biker could order up a hardtail frame, spoked wheels, springer fork and Mustang gas tank. Add engine and transmission, some bloody knuckles, rattle-can paint job and presto, one chopper assembled at home, often in the kitchen or spare bedroom.

Fast forward thirty years. Hardtails with raised necks and extended forks are once again all the rage. Only now the chopper styling can be combined with excellent engineering and aftermarket catalogs bursting with parts that are both well made and very stylish. Home-based bike builders never had it so good. Now you no longer have to cannibalize an existing bike to obtain an engine or transmission. Both are available from sources too numerous to list here. You can even buy a new engine of the same style used thirty years ago. Only this one is brand new, has more power than any V-twin built then, includes electronic ignition, a reliable carburetor and 32 amp charging system.

The goal of this book is to help you build a chopper – period. Twelve chapters cover History, Frames, Chassis Components, Wheels and Tires, Engine Options, Drivetrains, Wiring, Sheet Metal and Hardware. At the end of the book you find three assembly sequences photographed in professional shops. As always, we try to make you think first, before you run out to buy the coolest stuff.

This book is not a service manual. Which means you're going to have to buy one for things like torque specifications and help assembling some parts not covered here. If you're lucky enough to have a good aftermarket V-twin store nearby (what we used to call a chopper shop) it's a good idea to build a relationship with the crew there. No one knows more about building bikes than the people who build and repair them all day long. Before driving all over town for the best price on a billet caliper or primary assembly, consider that sometimes the information you learn from a good parts person is truly priceless.

To borrow a trite phrase, "this is not rocket science." Building a bike from scratch does involve careful attention to detail, however. In order to build a running bike you need a plan, the guts to follow it through, and the humility to ask for help or admit occasionally that "I don't know."

# Chapter One

# History

## A Little Perspective On All This Chopper Building

When people look back on the early days of customized Harleys, all they see are the psychedelic choppers from the 1970s. Panheads with long springer forks and metal-flake green paint jobs. What many of us forget is the fact that the choppers evolved from earlier motorcycles, and that those earlier bikes set the stage for the bikes we remember from the magazines and the movies.

The condensed version of chopper history

*This long chopper from Tom Rad (Rad Paint) is based on choppers from 1969 and 1970, what Tom calls, "the best years for choppers." Paughco frame is 5-1/2 ahead and 5 up with a 45 degree neck. Bobbed fender is from the aftermarket, Tom found an original Sportster tank, then added the blade and lowered the tunnel.*

might start after the second world war. Returning GIs came home and bought motorcycles - often the same bikes they saw during their time in Europe. Thus many of the bikes on the streets during the 1950s and 60s were not Harley-Davidsons, but Triumphs, BSAs and Royal Enfields.

Many of those early bikes were "customized" with a smaller gas tank, a smaller seat and a "Bates" headlight. The idea was to simplify the bikes, eliminate anything that wasn't necessary, and replace the necessary things like handle bars with parts that had more style.

The Harley guys were doing very similar things to their bikes, taking off anything that wasn't essential to the operation of the bike. By pulling the pin on the hinged fender a Harley rider could create an instant bobber. As Barry Cooney reports in his interview, riders were putting the longest of the factory forks on the front of their Harleys well before anyone coined the word chopper. Eventually, as bobbers became more popular and more radical they became known as choppers, bikes stripped of all but the barest essentials for operation.

All of this might be but a footnote in history if it hadn't been for one

*Engine is an 80 cubic inch model built on a Panhead bottom and Shovelhead top end with Weber carb. Transmission is an early style 4-speed. Note the king and queen seat with velvet insert, and bright pinstripes by Dave Bell.*

*Rear wheel measures 16 inches and carries a 5.00X16 Goodyear grasshopper. Straight laced front rim is wrapped by a mandatory Avon speedmaster. Tom used PPG candy tangerine sprayed over large metalflake base with panels in complimentary colors to create the effect seen here.*

certain movie. A movie that defined choppers and made Captain America bikes the preferred mode of expression for thousands of young American men.

So while we all remember the Peter Fonda bike, we've forgotten the fact that not all the bikes from those years looked like the perfect chopper. A scan through a series of old magazines from the late 1960s and early 1970s shows that the choppers, at least the ones in *Street Chopper* and *Chopper* and *Big Bike* and all the rest, weren't all Harley Panheads with flag paint jobs. What the magazines illustrate is the fact that there were Triumphs too numerous to count and even a fair number of Honda and Kawasaki four-cylinder choppers.

People did chop Harleys of course. But at least in the early days of choppers there were as many Sportsters as there were Big Twins. As local painter and Chopper enthusiast Tom Rad mentioned the other day, "The FL bikes were too expensive for most kids to own, most of us were lucky if we could afford an old Sportster."

Likewise the front forks, which were not all springers. Girders were very popular as were hydraulic forks. Length ranged from short and stock to too-long and really radical. Some carried front brakes while many did not. Handle bars ran the gamut from simple to too-tall and included Z-bars and the pull-backs made famous by Arlen Ness.

What defined a chopper depended on the year and the location. For some people a simple stripped Bonneville, Sportster or FL, what we might call a bobber or mild custom today, constituted a chopper. For others a chopper had to be a Harley and it had to have the signature items we associate with choppers today: Long springer fork, 74 inch V-twin, king and queen seat, tall sissy bar and a small Sportster or Mustang gas tank.

The formula for making choppers was – no formula. Then as now, what constituted a chopper was up to the rider. His vision, pocketbook and mechanical skills all helped determine the final form taken by the bike.

## CHOPPER SHOPS

The popularity of choppers created demand for frames and forks and all the rest, which in turn created a need for parts and someone to sell them. Thus was born an aftermarket industry with names like Amen, AEE, Jammer, Santee, SIE, D&D, Paughco and a dozen more. You could buy that hardtail frame (for $275.00) mail order or from the local chopper shop. While some chopper shops were little more than tiny retail outlets, some evolved into the

*Kendall Johnson built this chopper with a 40 degree hardtail frame, 4 inches up and 2 ahead. With 0-degree trees the trail is 4-1/2 inches. Fender and side covers are hand built, engine is one of Kendall's 113s. Wheels are his own "Killer Klown" brand, an 18 in back with a 250 tire, and a 21 in front.*

sophisticated businesses we know today as Custom Chrome and Drag Specialties.

As the industry grew their advertising dollars helped build the motorcycle press. And the press in turn promoted choppers, choppers and more choppers; built with two, three and four cylinders, rolling on two and often three wheels. There were no rules. Creative bikers built choppers from BMW twins and trikes from Volkswagen four bangers.

The bikes did change over the years, however. Harleys became the choppers of choice and eventually the Big Twin became the Harley to have. Short stubby choppers fell from favor, replaced by longer and longer bikes with more and more rake. Tanks no longer sat on the top tube, they seemed to grow out of the tube itself. In an effort to out-do the other guy, or please the judges at the shows, the bikes became wilder and wilder.

## FACTORY CHOPPERS

Fashions change and all things come to an end. By the early 1980s a series of events brought about the near extinction of choppers and custom bikes. One by one the chopper shops either closed or evolved into service facilities.

The death of choppers came about partly because of the soft American economy at the time. The other part of this sad story is the "factory customs" from Harley-Davidson that began to appear in the dealerships in about 1980 complete with extended forks, a 21 inch front tire, padded sissy bar and a red-on-black flamed paint job.

The 1980 Wide Glide was only the first in a long line of "custom" bikes built at the factory. After years of ignoring the styles and trends on main street, those same styles began to show up on the new bikes from Milwaukee. Ad copy for the Wide Glide called it a "California Classic," referring apparently to the birth place of the design.

For the die-hard chopper fans, things got worse before they got better. The aftermarket collapsed, the chopper magazines went away and the only ones making any money on motorcycles were the dealers.

The custom bike market did make a comeback in the late 1980s. Instead of long choppers though, the bikes of choice were Softails with trick paint and billet fender rails, or lowered FXRs with café fairings. Over the years as custom bikes became more and more sophisticated, and more expensive, a few individuals began to yearn for simpler bikes. Basic bikes. Bikes that were stripped or chopped. The spoked wheel never stops turning and what was passe' then is the hot

*Fully modern, this new chopper from Tuff Cycles uses a Gambler frame with 6 inches of stretch and a 46 degree neck. Forks are 12 over, equipped with dual brakes from JayBrake. S&S engine displaces 113 cubes, primary chain carries power to a 5 speed tranny, and by belt to the 180 rear tire.*

*Tuff Cycles used their own single downtube frame to create this nostalgia machine. "Swingarms are for girls," is the reason Tank gives for not offering this new frame in a soft-tail model. Engine is what Tank calls a hoochie coochie pan, an S&S lower end with STD heads.*

*Hallcraft straight laced wheels measure 18 and 21 inches, rear Avon is stamped 200X18, unique primary cover houses a 4 inch Karata belt. Wrap around fenders are from D&D, unique tank started as a mini-bike tank before being stretched by the Tuff guy.*

ticket now. Through 360 degrees we roll, back to where we were thirty years ago.

Only now we have a very sophisticated aftermarket to provide every imaginable frame, fender, engine and taillight for your new chopper. Long, short, raw or smooth, you can have that new chopper in any form you desire. Want it cheap? Buy a basic hardtail frame, equip it with simple wire wheels, hydraulic forks, an 80 inch Evo engine and five speed transmission.

Really want to make a statement? Buy a long stretched soft-tail type frame, add the springer fork, 240 spoke wheels, 250 rear tire, hand formed gas tank, 120 cubic inch polished engine and six speed transmission. Now send all the parts out to a well known painter for a trick candy or flamed paint job.

The rule is, there are no rules. Some choppers are long and some are short, some are hardtails and some are soft. This isn't to say that one is good and the other is bad. All are good, but one might be better for you.

## INTERVIEW: BARRY COONEY

*Though Barry Cooney gave up his chopper shop years ago, he still builds custom motorcycles, just a few each year in his well equipped home shop. Barry doesn't brag, he just shows up each year in Sturgis with another new bike built from a combination of aftermarket parts and hand fabricated goodies. Each bike, whether a rubber-ride or soft-tail chopper, is well designed, exhibits incredible attention to detail, and runs hard down Spearfish Canyon Highway. Barry was there in the beginning and he's still there today.*

*Barry, let's start with some background on you..*

I was always a car and bike guy. As soon as I turned 16 I had a hot rod, a 1931 Ford Roadster with a hopped up flathead. My first bike was a Matchless I bought when I was 18. Then I went through the whole gamut of English bikes and did all types of racing, flat-track and TT, motocross and enduro, drag race and road race.

Eventually I got turned on to Harleys, I made the turn about the time of the *Easy Rider* movie. In 1971 opened my bike shop in Portland, Oregon, we called it BC Choppers.

*Can you tell us a little about the shop and the kinds of bikes you were building?*

Well, 50 percent of my customers were riding Panheads, 20 percent were on Knuckles the rest were on Shovels. The go-fast guys were putting big Sportster engines in rigid frames.

Some of the bikes that we built in our shop were longer and lower than other bikes of the period. I liked that street racer look. But we also built lots of very traditional Panhead choppers. You couldn't just go out and buy a custom frame easily in those days so mostly we used dog-leg or straight-leg Harley frames. The hot deal was a straight leg Panhead frame from 1955 to

1957. We cut them up and raked them, cut off all the mounting tabs. The antique guys say there aren't any stock frames left, that's because we cut them all up! In 1981 I sold the shop because things were getting mighty slim. Only the strong ones survived the '80s and made it into the '90s and the current wave of popularity for Harleys. Guys like Arlen Ness who had a strong biker customer base in the bay area. The guys I sold the shop to made it two more years.

*Where did the term chopper come from?*

After the war, guys would take the back of the rear fender off at the hinge. Those were initially called bob jobs, trim the rear fender and throw away the front fender. Gradually in early '50s it was said you were "chopping them up." The bikes went from being a bob job to a chopper.

*When did the long front ends get popular, and what about the raised necks?*

For the most part when all this got started there were none of these long front ends. Just stock springers or wide glide forks. The way it started, some guys would put on the springer

*Bruce Bush (Wizard Custom Painting outside Minneapolis, MN) calls this, "a good old barn find." Built mostly out of the Jammer catalogue, the bike uses a hardtail frame with their twisted springer fork, 16 and 19 inch rims. Built in 1969 the engine uses a 1960 XLCH powerplant.*

*Barry Cooney's bike is based on a Daytec frame with 40 degrees of rake and zero-degree trees. Fork assembly is from Arlen Ness, a wide glide assembly with torpedo lower legs. Sixty spoke wheels are from Roadwings, rear tire is a 200.*

*By mounting the rear fender to the frame Barry was able to "get it down there" and help maintain the look and the lines of a hardtail chopper. Open belt primary from Primo is part of that look as well.*

from the WLR, the military bike. Those forks were two inches longer than a regular fork and people thought those were pretty cool.

Then someone came up with the idea of using wishbones from an old Model A Ford suspension to extend the fork. That was how the first long front ends came about. But the first choppers didn't have those long forks. If you look at the movie the *Wild Angels*, the bikes are almost all short bikes with stock wide glide or springer forks, upswept pipes and risers with drag bars. That is what choppers really looked like back in the '60s.

When they started putting on the long forks though the bikes were getting jacked up really high and the motor was way off the ground. Some guys would really rake the frame to get the bike back down closer to the ground but then they were floppy to ride. Or else you had to raise the neck.

*How about sheet metal, give us an idea the type of tank and fenders a typical chopper from the period might have.*

We didn't have big catalogs to choose the parts from. You could either use English style fenders with the raised rib in the center, or five or six inch flat steel fenders. If you wanted something different you had to make it. I used a 5.60X15 car tire on the back of one of my bikes, mounted on a 12 spoke American Mag wheel. I needed a real wide fender so I took a stock Sporty rear fender, cut the skirt off, widened it and then leaded the lip so it had a nice clean edge. You made stuff, that's what you had to do. Most bikes had Sportster tanks or peanut tanks. Guys would change the tunnel so the tank sat higher on the tube.

*How practical were most of those bikes?*

Not very. You didn't want to ride at the back of the pack because of all the parts falling off the other bikes. Traveling to someplace like Sturgis was an excuse to fix bikes by the side of the road in another state.

*You just built a new chopper, can you tell us a little about your new bike?*

The bike is a blend of old and new. It's a soft-tail style frame with disc brakes and electric start – which of course we didn't have in the old days. This bike has the rigid look, and I mounted the rear fender on the swingarm so the fender is right down there on the tire, that's the only way to get that good look. The rear tire is a 200, that isn't a real wide tire anymore, but it's a whole lot wider than what we used to have. I like the bike, it sits like a rigid.

Russ Wernimont made the gas tank, and we modified one of his rear fenders. The Daytec frame has 40 degrees of rake with two inches of stretch in the back bone and five in the downtubes. The wide glide trees are from Arlen, they don't have any rake and the

bike works well, it doesn't have any front end flop even at low speeds. The motor is square, a 4X4 from S&S for a total of 100 cubic inches. With the short stroke there's less vibration. It's a good compromise, big enough to have some power and still pretty smooth which is important, especially in a soft-tail frame with a solid mounted engine. I put on a 45 mm side draft Webber carburetor for that chopper-hot rod look. The primary is open with a three inch belt from Primo. I fabricated everything else.

*Any final comments on choppers now and then?*

The bikes are safer and easier to ride now, therefore there are a lot of new riders and some of them are riding choppers. They think it's all about fun, and it *is* fun, if you pay attention and learn to ride well. Many however, don't seem to realize that people can get seriously hurt on bikes, it's not a game.

*Barry Cooney was building choppers when they were first discovered, and he's still building… and riding them today.*

## Chapter Two

# The Chopper Frame

## And Related Issues

Rather than make this chapter a Buyer's Guide for chopper frames, we've decided to simply talk about frames and frame issues: What they are, the different styles, what they're made of and how to pick a frame that's right for your project.

### WHAT'S A CHOPPER?

As humans we often seem prone to conflict. Whether it's religion or politics or motorcycles, the emphasis is on our differences rather than any kind of common ground. A good example: the Harley or

*This sanitary chopper is from David Perewitz and the Cycle Fab crew. Ape hangers work well, the Daytec frame is only 2 up and 2 out with a 38 degree neck and 0-degree trees. Sheet metal is hand made in-house. 80 spoke wheels from Hallcraft look right at home on this chopper. Rear Wheel carries a 200X16 Avon. Dino Petracelli*

Honda debate that still rages through the saloons and campgrounds where ever two-wheeled enthusiasts gather.

Choppers are no different. We tend to think that all the real choppers came with Panhead engines stuffed into hardtail frames with twenty-over springer forks. Yet, if you read the old issues of *Street Chopper*, you find choppers with 650cc Triumph engines or even (heresy here) 900cc Kawasaki mills, along with plenty of Harley-Davidsons. Some had long springer forks, but just as many used hydraulic front ends, and some of those weren't even extended. The Neo choppers are nearly all based on Harley engines. Does that mean that my friend Bob's period-correct Honda 750 isn't a chopper? Or that a twin-shock frame can't be used as the basis of a Chopper?

For the purposes of this book we've taken a more inclusive attitude. The bikes presented here are powered by American V-Twin engines set into hardtail or soft-tail style frames. That doesn't mean you can't use an old Triumph 650 engine for power, or that you have to have 50 degrees of rake and a 21 inch front wheel. Choppers are about attitude, about breaking the rules, about making a very personal statement.

You can build anything you want and call it a chopper. We have assembled this book around the idea that you are building a chopper from scratch rather than building one out of an existing bike. Most of the frames presented here are of the two styles described above, often with the necessary raised neck and additional rake.

*Another Perewitz creation based on another Daytec frame, this one with a 40 degree neck that's 5 up and 2 out, with 3-degree trees. Fork is a 10-over Perewitz assembly. Spoked wheels are from Ness, rear tire measures 200, brakes by JayBrake. D. Petracelli*

*Choppers need belt drive and this bike uses a belt and pulleys from Jerry Covington. 107 cubic inch engine is from TP Engineering, 5-speed transmission carries the same logo. Perewitz coil bracket with ignition switch helps to make for a simple wiring harness. D. Petracelli*

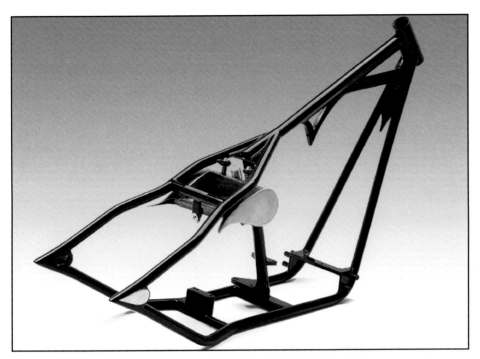

*This new "Stray Kat" frame from Cyril Huze accepts 250 rear tires with a 1-1/2 inch belt. Built from Chrome moly for strength, this new frame combines classic chopper lines with Cyril's own unique details like the teardrop oil tank and axle covers.*

*Some soft-tail style frames make better hardtails that others. This one, designed by Donnie Smith, moves the pivot inboard and has a swingarm that blends into the frame tubing under the seat. CSI*

A good chopper exudes a certain raw energy even while at rest. Part of that energy is created by the radical design. By getting more radical though you don't always get more energy. A fifty degree rake angle may be cool but that doesn't mean a seventy degree rake is even cooler. At some point the bikes become freakish, or at least very difficult to ride on a regular basis.

Which brings up a good point. These are motorcycles not designer jeans or objects of art. The initial idea was to strip or chop the motorcycle, and thus bring it back to the bare essentials. One frame, two wheels and one engine; with just enough sheet metal to hold some gas. Thus built, the bikes were lighter, faster and handled better (handling being a relative term here). Peter Fonda just looked so damned cool riding that long Panhead that every red-blooded American kid had to have one and we've kind of forgotten where it all started.

So build yourself the coolest F-ing chopper the world has ever seen. Remember though that at some point you may want to ride it more than five miles to the local show or the corner tap. Buy good components, put on some brakes, stop short of being so radical that the bike is unstable at speed or just plain dangerous. If you've never built a chopper before, ask around to ensure your combination of components, the rake and triple trees will provide you with a rideable two-wheeled platform (for more on building a rideable bike see the interview with Donnie Smith).

## DESIGN THE BIKE

A quick look at the choppers in a current issue of *Street Chopper* illustrates the fact that even within this narrow motorcycle niche, there's plenty of room for individual expression. Choppers range from short bobber-type machines to the long radical rides. Use one of CCI's new soft-tail Kodlin frames for a modern European look or a Pat Kennedy frame as the basis for a very traditional chop.

Engine choices include Knuckleheads, Panheads and Shovelheads (both old and new), Evos (from Milwaukee or the aftermarket) and the new TC engine from Milwaukee (more on engines in Chapter Five).

Unless you're buying one of the kits available from the aftermarket (more later) you need to think all this through before buying parts. You need a picture of what the new bike will look like, either a real photo or clippings from a magazine. Creative types might do a complete sketch or rendering of the bike. If free-hand art isn't your forte', take photos of a bike similar to what you intend to build. Run up to the local copy store and make some cheap black and white enlargements. With scissors and tape you can easily change the position of the neck or the rake angle.

How you decide what to build isn't important, but you do need to decide what the bike will look like before ordering parts. Too many first-time builders are disappointed with their finished machine because they didn't put enough effort in on the

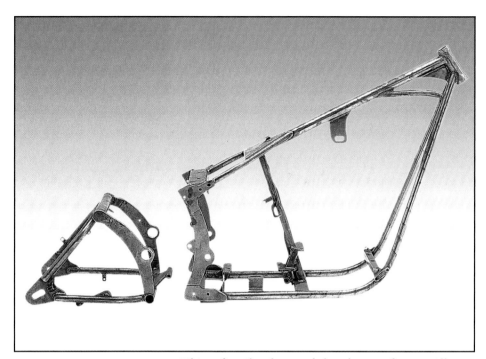

*This soft-tail style stretch leg chopper frame will accept a 200 series tire. Comes with 4 inches of downtube stretch and 3-1/2 of top tube stretch. Designed for Evo drivetrain, the frame is manufactured from 1-1/8 inch mild steel tubing. Biker's Choice*

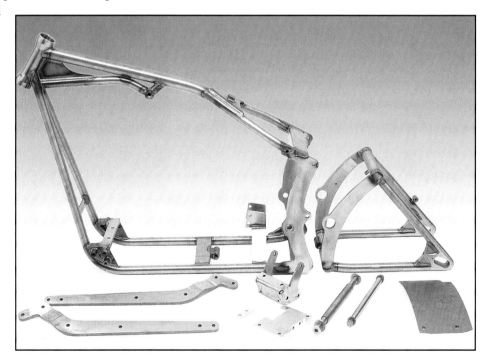

*There are some frames out there designed for Sportster powerplants. This example uses 35 degrees of rake and no stretch to create a compact soft-tail powered by a 883 or 1200 engine with a 180 rear tire. Biker's Choice*

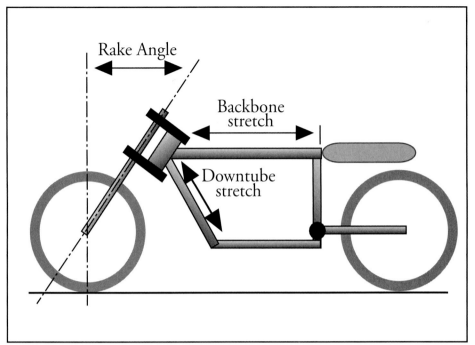

*We now have two kinds of stretch, in the top tube and the downtubes. On the street people talk about a certain frame as having, "a 38 degree neck that's "3 ahead and 4 up."*

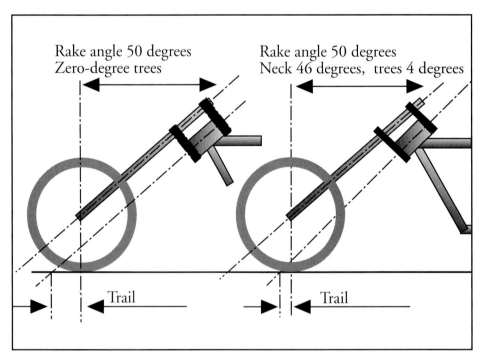

*Many experienced chopper builders get part of their total rake from the trees, as a way to reduce the trail and thus some of the heavyness that comes with extreme rake angles.*

front end. During the mock-up stage you can make adjustments that affect the look of the bike, but by then it's too late to do a compete redesign.

## THE RIGHT FRAME

We've said all this before, but it bears repeating: The frame is the foundation of your machine and must be chosen with care. You need to first pick the look or design of the bike. Is this going to be a stubby early-style chopper with short dimensions and a 30 degree neck, or one of the long extended bikes with raised neck and extended fork? Once you have the basic idea down on paper you can shop for a frame that will provide the look you're trying to achieve. You also need to consider the size of the rider. A former NBA player needs different dimensions than a biker who's five foot six.

You need a high quality frame. This is the one part of the bike that nearly everything else attaches to. If the frame isn't straight, for whatever reason, no amount of fixing or adjusting will make it right. Though most aftermarket frames are high-quality products, some are better than others. We suggest you ask around in the local shops to see which frames they prefer and why.

## TERMS

Before delving further into a discussion of frames, it might be helpful to define some terms. Rake is the angle of the fork assembly when compared to vertical. When it comes to choppers the rake at the neck may be different than the rake of the fork itself, done in an effort to control the trail.

## RAKE AND TRAIL

Trail is the distance between the front tire's contact patch and the point where the centerline of the bike's steering axis meets the ground (see the illustrations). Motorcycles have positive trail. Much like the caster angle of an automobile, positive trail provides the straight line stability that allows us to take our hands off the bars while going down the road.

Many people think rake and trail are essentially the same. Wrong. However, with most standard-issue front fork assemblies and standard triple trees an increase in rake *will* result in an increase in positive trail. With choppers this means a rake angle of 45 degrees can result in a trail dimension of eight or more inches.

Choppers can end up with way too much trail and that really heavy feeling when turning at slow speeds. Many experienced chopper builders will buy a frame with 42 degrees of rake and then use a set of three-degree trees for a total of 45 degrees of rake. By using the three-degree trees they reduce the trail to a more manageable level (like roughly four to five inches) and get rid of that really heavy feeling, sometimes known as "flop" (for more on trail see the comments in Chapter Three.)

## STRETCH

The current popularity of choppers and bikes with raised necks means that we have two types of "stretch." Typical stretch refers to mater-

*The kit concept is hot, as evidenced by this complete BYOB kit (the Spitfire) from CCI. At least ten different complete bikes are now offered. Just add labor and paint.*

*This early style wishbone frame from Santee will accept Evo or earlier engines, and 4 speed transmissions with chain final drive. CCI*

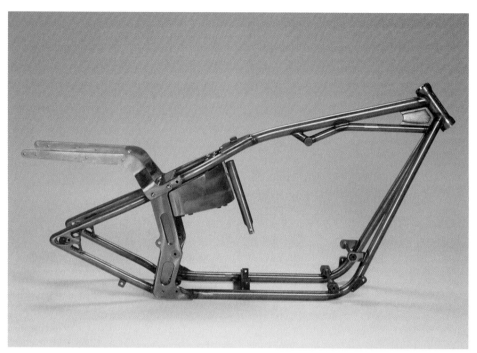

*This Ness-Tail 250 frame is designed to accept the TC 88 (shown) or Evo engines. With a one inch off-set kit or offset transmission assembly, these frames will accept a ten inch wide rear tire. Arlen Ness*

*This EZ Widener kit makes it easy to install a 200 series tire in a Softail frame. Kit includes swingarm, transmission plate, primary spacer, offset engine sprocket and assorted hardware. Biker's Choice*

ial added to the top tube – sometimes called a stretched backbone. Downtube stretch refers to the material added to the downtubes to raise the neck. People used to say a frame was "stretched two inches" meaning it's two inches longer between the seat and the neck than it was originally (or than a similar factory frame). Now, when you ask a frame builder about the dimensions of a new frame they might say it's, "three inches ahead and two inches up," meaning the neck is positioned three inches ahead and two inches higher than a "stock" frame.

## How To Choose the Right One

The frame decision will affect and be affected by your choice of an engine and your feelings on style and the way you will use the bike. First you need to decide where you want the shocks, or if there should be any shocks at all. Once you've decided on the basic frame type you need to find the individual frame that's right for your project. Before buying an aftermarket frame you need to talk to some builders and shops in your area because the quality of aftermarket frames ranges from very good to not-so-great. The people who know the difference are the ones building bikes day in and day out.

Though most builders want more radical designs, there are some near-copies of factory soft-tail and FXR frames on the market. Not only are these frames often less expensive to buy, they are generally less expensive to equip as well. These chassis will accept stock hardware and sheet metal, which tends to be the least expensive to buy new and the most commonly seen at the swap meet.

When you buy a frame remember that some are fairly raw and have no mounting bosses for the Fat Bob tanks. This translates into more work and/or money. Many frame manufacturers offer a build sheet, much like the option list available when you buy a new car. With this sheet you can often specify dimensions and the type of tank mounting system you require.

## BUY QUALITY

When it comes to buying a quality frame there are a number of important points to consider. As Arlen Ness explained years ago, you need a frame that's straight, but there's more to it than that: "You need to be sure everything is straight and true. All the parts should bolt to the frame without you having to take a rat-tail file to the holes. Look for high quality welds. Some shops don't do a very good job of fitting the tubes together. Where one tube fits to another they don't do a nice concave cutout. The fit is poor so they just fill the gap up with weld material.

"If you buy a cheap frame and the welds are rough, and you have to mold the welds, you might end up spending more money than if you bought the more expensive frame in the first place. We try to have frames with really nice welds so you don't have to do any molding."

## MATERIALS

Most of the aftermarket frames are constructed from mild steel, a few use chrome-moly tubing. As the owner of one fabrication shop explained, "For most of these frames, no one did a computerized engineering study. They didn't do a material analysis of mild steel, they chose it because experience taught them that mild steel tubing, of a certain quality in a certain size and wall thickness, was plenty strong enough."

Though chrome-moly might be the stronger material you can't simply say that chrome-moly frames are better than those built from mild steel. Chrome moly requires better welding techniques, and is less forgiving when two tubes don't meet perfectly. And while chrome moly may result in a lighter frame, weight isn't an issue for most of the choppers we build. Pat Kennedy adds the comment that "To me a chopper is a long bike, and the extra length and extra rake put more stress on the frame and the neck area in particular. So what's good enough for most frames may not be good enough for a chopper frame."

## THE MOCK-UP
### Before you bolt it together

Professional shops build their motorcycles twice. Once in the raw and once for real. The reasons for doing a mock up of the bike with raw components are numerous. First, you get to see how the bike is actually going to look. By bolting on the tank(s), fender and seat you can see how the bike looks and whether or not you like the new lines and the way all the components work together in a visual sense. This requires that you set up the bike at ride height and that your work area is large enough to get back from

*This adjustable triple tree allows for adjustments in rake so you can have the ideal trail figure, even if you alter the bike from the original configuration. Available for 41 and 39mm fork tubes. Cyril Huze*

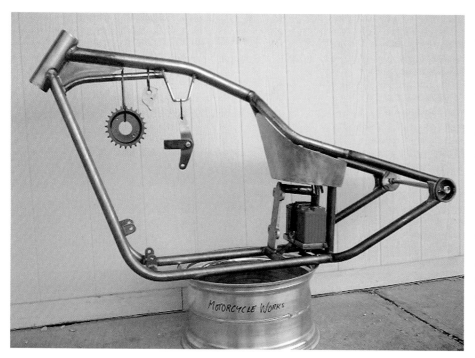

*This unique "drop-seat" frame is designed to accommodate a Sportster engine. Available in two versions, a 200 and 240 rear tire. Rakes all the way to 42 degrees. Built from DOM mild steel tubing. Motorcycle Works*

*This is the basis of most "wide tire kits" for soft-tail style frames: one spacer that goes between the engine and inner primary, an offset engine sprocket, a pulley spacer and an offset transmission plate. Biker's Choice*

the bike far enough to see it as you will when it's parked outside. If the garage is small you might put the work bench on wheels or roll the mock up outside so you can be back far enough from the bike to make honest judgments about the lines and proportions of the parts.

Perhaps more important than being able to see how the bike looks is the check to see how the various components actually fit the frame and each other. This is the time to weld brackets to the frame or enlarge a hole in the fender so it bolts correctly to the strut. You don't want to discover the need for a bracket or new hole after all the parts come back from the paint shop.

Part of checking the fit of all the parts includes a thorough examination to ensure that when the suspension moves through the full range of motion, especially when it bottoms, that fenders and brackets can't possibly touch the tires. Remember that when you bottom the bike on a rough road the suspension probably moves slightly past what appears to be the "stop." The best builders and fabricators anticipate a worst-case scenario by using smooth button-head bolts under the fender that screw up or away from the tire to hold on the fender. People also forget that when they lower the bike two inches that means the bike is two inches closer to the pavement when the suspension hits bottom. Make sure the frame rails can't hit the ground over rough pavement.

And while we all like to see fenders set down close to the tire, you can overdo this good thing. The problem is the fact that tires grow in size as speed increases, thus diminishing the clearance. To quote Craig from Hoppe and Associates, the Avon distributor: "Tire clearance is a big issue. People don't take into account the growth at speed. I tell people they need one inch of vertical clearance, that's a good guideline. You can still get the fender to wrap the tire nicely. This is even more of a problem when there's less pressure in the tire, like on hardtails where they run the tire a little soft so the ride isn't as harsh. I say, 'make allowances,' if in doubt consult the manufacturer's customer service people."

Finally, don't miss the obvious trouble areas. Make sure the clips on the inside of some fenders, intended to hold the taillight wires, can't touch the side of tire. The other obvious trouble spot is the bolt or pin assembly used to hold down the back of the seat. Be sure the tire can't touch this bolt, or eliminate it altogether by using two strips of hook-and-loop fastener to hold the back of the seat in place.

## FRAMES IN THE REAL WORLD
### Hardtails:

As the name implies, a hardtail frame uses no rear suspension. These frames are simpler to manufacture and thus may offer an inexpensive entry into the scratch-built chopper market. The lack of suspension means a hardtail frame can be the foundation for a strictly-business kind of hot rod machine. Hardtail frames have those great lines, the look of a classic V-twin motorcycle. The down side is the fact that these can in fact be hard on your rear end and back.

There are a number of interesting alternatives for builders seeking these very simple frame designs. In addition to rake angles, you can buy your hardtail frame "stretched" in either – often both – dimensions. Some hardtails come with a "wishbone" shape in the front downtubes, and some provide for rubber-mounted engines. A few of these frames mimic

*A step beyond standard soft-tail style frames, this Streetster from Paul Yaffe features hidden axles, pointed accents, and flush mount pivots. Available in Evo (shown) or TC models, these frames are fabed from chrome moly. Also comes in a chopper version with 6 inches of up-stretch. CCI*

*Kit from Santee makes room for 200 series tires through use of wider swingarm and a standard "wide tire kit" to move the transmission to the left. CSI*

*Professional shops build a bike at least twice, once in mock up stage and once after all the parts have been painted and polished. Cyril Huze*

*You can't just screw together most of the bike, you need to assemble the whole thing. Including the drivetrain and exhaust. Cyril Huze*

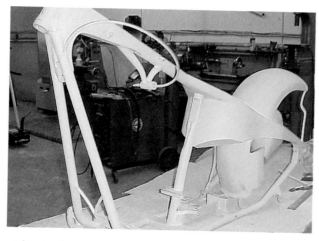

*After he knows everything fits it's time to remove the engine and transmission and all the rest and start preparations for paint. Cyril Huze*

the dimensions of the early Harley-Davidson frames, like the hardtail frames from Edlund that include the sidecar mounts. Most of the modern hardtails will accept any Big Twin engine including the new TC 88B. New designs with wider rear sections allow you to use the currently popular 230, 240 and 250 rear tires with belt drive. If the hardtail you've sketched out on paper uses a 230 series rear tire and a five-speed transmission, be sure the frame you buy will accommodate those design criteria.

While the traditional hardtail frame includes the welded in center post between the engine and transmission, newer designs delete that post (or use a bolt-in post) a necessity for any chassis that accepts the unitized TC 88 engine and transmission from H-D. As mentioned elsewhere a TC 88 engine (the non-B version) can be mated up to an earlier style five-speed transmission with the use of an adapter plate on the back of the engine. A TC 88B however, needs to be mated up to a transmission designed specifically for that engine.

Recent innovations in the hardtail department include single downtube frames from West Coast Choppers, Thunder Cycle and Tuff Cycle (to mention only three) most of which can be ordered in almost any combination of stretch and rake. Thunder Cycles can even match up one of their chopper frames with their single-sided swingarm.

**Soft-tail style frames**

By far the most popular frame ever conceived for a V-Twin engine is the one that looks like a hardtail while providing a certain amount of suspension travel. The best of both worlds you might say, the soft-tail frame bolts the engine and transmission directly into the frame (as God intended) and provides the lines that only a hardtail can offer.

Prior to the introduction of the TC 88 engine, nearly all soft-tail style frames used a center post, and bolted the engine to two pads located ahead of the post, and the transmission to similar pads behind the post, with an additional bracket on the transmission's right side. Daytec was one of the first to install a plate for mounting the transmission, instead of two pads, thus strengthening the frame.

Many of these soft-tail style frames come with the transmission mounting holes already offset, eliminating the need for an offset plate, and a wider rear section and matching swingarm, to accommodate the ten inch rubber.

If you want to make a chopper out of a twin shock frame, either new from the aftermarket, or as manufactured by Harley-Davidson in many models, there's no one here to tell you no. Because the vast majority of choppers use either hardtail or soft-tail style frames however, we've included only those two styles in our overview of the frame market.

## PHAT TIRES

Most frame styles are available with a wide rear section to accommodate wide rear tires. You definitely need to decide how wide the rear tire should be during the planning phase, as the width of the rear tire will affect your choice of a frame, rear fender, and wheel to mention only three of the items on the list of stuff to buy.

Installing a wide rear tire, by wide we mean 200 series and up, generally means use of an offset kit to move the transmission and possibly the engine to the left to make room between the belt (or chain) and the tire. Option number two is the use of a transmission with right side drive, which puts the final drive belt on the other side and requires little or no offset, resulting in better-balanced motorcycle.

Chapter Five goes into the drivetrain options in more detail. You will however, have to decide on the rear wheel dimensions before you spend hard-earned cash for a frame.

## SWINGARMS
### Fat Tires for Skinny Frames

Note: Most of this book is based on the premise that you are building a chopper based on a new frame. For anyone starting with an existing soft-tail style frame though we've included the following discussion.

You don't have to buy a complete frame in order to run a wide rear tire. The aftermarket does supply extra wide swingarms that allow you to mount a 180, 200 or 230 series tire, and belt drive, in stock and near-stock frames.

Harley-Davidson even has a kit that allows you to run a wider rear tire in a late-model Softail chassis. There are actually two kits, for pre and post-2000 model Softails, that allows the owner to swap the stock 130 series rear tire for a 150 series tire from Dunlop. These kits create the necessary clearance between belt and tire through the use of a narrower belt and appropriate rear pulley.

A more common approach to adding the wide tire to a stock frame is taken by the X-Drive designed by Donnie Smith and sold by Chrome Specialties (a very similar kit is offered by Custom Chrome) for pre-2000 year Softails and similar frames from the aftermarket.

By moving the swingarm's left side support to the inside and routing the belt *between* the frame and the swingarm, the X-Drive swingarm allows the use of a tire that's 7-5/8 inches across. Note: the width of the tire depends on both the tire brand and the width of the rim it's mounted on. Also found in the Custom Chrome catalog are some European swingarms meant for soft-tail style frames. With a style all their own, these swingarms allow the use of a 200 series tire and standard 1-1/2 inch belt, or a wider tire when combined with a narrow belt or chain. And so

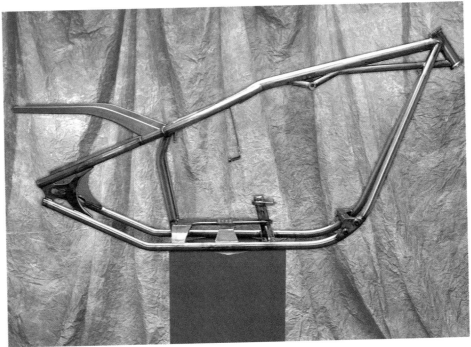

*Part of the Donnie Smith signature series, this Evo-style hardtail frame eliminates the center post for a clean look. Built from mild steel tubing in various rake and stretch dimensions. CSI*

*Rolling chassis kits offer certain advantages beyond price. You know the fenders and tank fit and that the fork assembly wheels and tires will produce a level bike. This kit from Biker's Choice can be ordered with engine, transmission and primary drive.*

we're not accused of playing favorites, PM, Biker's Choice, J&P and Drag Specialties offer wide tire swingarm kits as well.

## KITS, KITS, KITS

The hot ticket in frames isn't just the frames themselves, but rather the components that come along with the chassis and swingarm. Everyone from Dave Perewitz to American Thunder to CCI (Custom Chrome Inc.) and Biker's Choice offer frame kits that include at least the sheet metal, at most everything you need to build the bike.

The kit concept eliminates questions about how long the fork tubes should be to produce a level bike, or which dash components to buy with the fat bob tanks. American Thunder sells their "rollers" with fork assembly, wheels, tires, fenders, tank(s) and forward controls (one of our assembly sequences seen at the back of the book is a American Thunder kit). Biker's choice has their Bike In A Box kits, and CCI offers complete B.Y.O.B. (build your own bike) kits that include everything but the paint and assembly labor. They even offer financing.

Like buying a set of tools from Sears, the companies offering the kits for sale have set the price of the package lower than the typical cost to go out and buy the components separately. The bigger advantage might simply be the fact that the kits eliminate the hassle of deciding which fenders and which tank and how should they be mounted (a bigger considera-

*Owned by John Malone, this is the finished product of all the work seen on page 27. Definitely a new chopper, John's bike uses a 230X15 rear tire and 21 inch front tire. Long hydraulic fork is mounted in zero-degree trees.*

tion for the tanks). When it comes to kits, you can buy a very simple near-copy of a factory Softail from CCI or Biker's Choice (and others as well), or a radical right-side-drive bike with 250 rear tire from Dave Perewitz or American Thunder.

The same ground rules apply to buying a kit as buying a bare frame. Is it a quality piece from a well known manufacturer? Is there technical support on the other end of an 800 number to answer your questions? Do they offer a warranty against defects? What kind of compromises in rear tire and engine location were made to accommodate a wide tire?

The bike you build needs to satisfy only one person. Figure out what you want, what it is you're trying to accomplish in building this new bike, and then pick a quality frame and related components that help you do exactly that.

## TITLE CONSIDERATIONS

When you build a motorcycle from scratch based on a Kennedy frame, it will be titled as a Kennedy, not as a Harley-Davidson. Many states will title a scratch-built bike as "special construction" much like a reconstructed vehicle, a car or motorcycle that's been rebuilt from a wreck. What follows are general guidelines for the process of obtaining a title.

Many states require you to bring the bike to the state Motor Vehicle Testing Station for an inspection. A few states make it very difficult to register a scratch-built bike. Each state is a little different so take the time before you start on the project to call the state to inquire exactly what they require. Also ask them to FAX you the legal requirements for a motorcycle i.e., horn, turnsignals etc.

When you buy a frame, engine cases, or a complete engine from any legitimate aftermarket supplier you will get a MSO (Manufacturers Statement of Origin). Be sure it is filled out correctly and that any previous transfers are noted. If the paper work isn't clean don't buy the parts. Before providing a title for a scratch-built bike most states require that you provide them with the MSO with serial numbers noted for both the engine cases and the frame.

A complete used engine might not be such a hot deal, unless you buy it from a reputable dealer who can provide the necessary paperwork. It's also not a good idea to base your new engine on a set of used Harley-Davidson cases. Without a MSO the state probably won't give you a title for the new bike.

*The start of the project, a Rolling Thunder hardtail frame with a 40 degree neck, 6 up and 5 out. Tank and fender were mounted by Neal Letourneau.*

*Though John did his own assembly, the mock up was done at the Kokesh MC shop. Rear fender is from Russ Wernimont, the stretched steel tank is from Independent. Oil tank is part of the frame kit.*

*The engine in John's beast is a big inch V-twin assembled with Axtel cast iron cylinders. Three inch belt will pass power to the RevTech 6-speed tranny. Final drive is by chain with an Exile caliper squeezing the rear sprocket.*

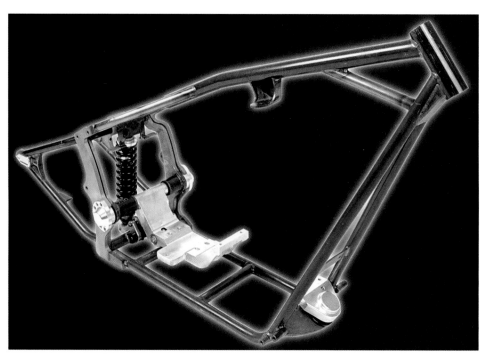

*The Roadster frames built by Paul Yaffe mount the soft-tail type drive train in rubber to produce a smooth ride equal to a FXR or Dresser. Note the single shock rear suspension. Accepts a 200 tire with belt, built from chrome moly tubing. CCI*

*This wishbone frame from Paughco comes with 2-1/4 inches of stretch in the top tube and will accept Evo or earlier engines. Flatside tank mounts installed. Designed for 4 speed transmissions and chain drive. Biker's Choice*

You have to convince the authorities that sales tax has been paid on all the parts used to build the motorcycle, and that the parts came from legitimate sources. Don't buy new cases, which come with the necessary MSO, and then fill them with "used" internals, unless you can supply good paper work for the pistons and 'wheels and all the rest.

Get receipts when you can, especially for big-ticket items. If the price of a used part seems too good to be true, ask yourself why. Before taking advantage of those "special prices" consider that without a market there would be very little theft.

Professional shops suggest you keep perfect records and paperwork and a duplicate file in case the file you turn in is lost. Keep a photo record, for your own enjoyment and to prove to the authorities that you really did screw this bike together yourself. As each state has their own rules, which are subject to change, advice from a local bike builder can be very useful and help you navigate the legalities of getting title for your new hot rod.

## INTERVIEW:
## PAT KENNEDY

*When most of the bikers in the United States gave up their choppers back in the early 1980s, there was one who refused to conform. While the rest of us took up rubber-mounts with café fairings or Softails with billet fender rails and stretched tanks, one man kept the vigil. For Pat Kennedy choppers are the only true motorcycles. They are in fact more than motorcycles. If there is one man with the balls to follow the beat of his own distant drummer, that man is Pat Kennedy.*

*Pat, how about some background on you. How long have you been involved with motorcycles and with choppers?*

Really, I've been involved with motorcycles my whole life. As a youth, when the other kids wanted to be firemen or doctors I wanted to be a biker. This was never a weekend deal. I've had no other job. I've been in it my whole life. I have two older brothers, five and ten years older than myself and they had bikes. Motorcycles were always there. I built my first motorcycle for a guy when I was in the sixth grade. I've ridden other bikes, I rode dirt bikes and did some racing as a kid but none of those I would consider a real motorcycle.

I only consider choppers to be motorcycles. There is nothing else there for me. That's where my mind is. I do look at all bikes though. I love all the aspects of the bike world, even bicycles. I studied bicycle racers to learn about rake and trail.

To me choppers are so far beyond motorcycle, it's a feeling, it's a life. I've ridden with guys all over the world and been to other places in the world where choppers were popular. I walk into a club in Japan or France and they understand what I'm doing. Even though they can't speak my language and I can't speak theirs.

I have a background in machining, welding and painting. You get to that point in your life where you want to know as much as you can about what you're creating. I consider chopper building to be an art, craftsmanship and something beyond that. That's why I've never been in the main stream. I cater to people who come to me and say, 'this is what I've wanted my whole life.'

I don't mass produce anything, That's not the niche I'm after. I build and have ridden choppers for 25 years. I still do it. I don't build like anybody else, my bikes look like I built them. I build a small line of parts. Adjustable front ends, wheels, tanks and frames that the average builder can use to go in and get a start on a bike.

*Tell us a little bit about your frames, the basic models and what the frames are made from?*

For most of the years I built rigid frames. Now I make a suspension frame but these aren't normal as far as the typical soft-tail frame goes. Mine are not copies of a Harley frame that got stretched and modified. I built a frame and then I drove it and changed what I didn't like and exaggerated what I did like. My rigid frames are the same way, in terms of coming up with a design and improving it through riding and use.

If you looked at most factory bikes, none have zero aligned wheels, they have some offset. My wheels are centered and in line, and the motor is centered on the centerline. I only move the transmission so the belt will clear the rear tire, I never offset the engine. I built some drag racing frames and saw what happened with offset engines. About

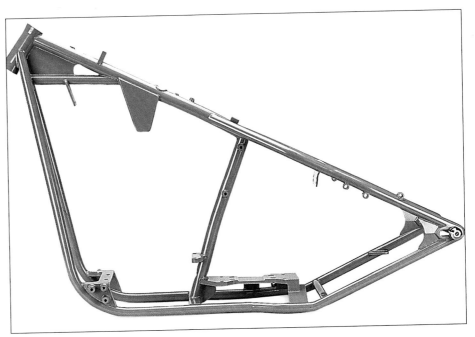

*By stretching the downtubes 4 inches, the builders at Daytec have created a chopper frame with a straight backbone. Accepts 200 tire with full-size belt, Note the integral transmission mounting plate. Biker's Choice*

six feet off the line they would pitch off to one side and then the bike was never straight again the rest of the way down the track.

I use chrome moly for all the frames. When I first started building frames I wanted the strength and durability, even if it is a more finicky material to work with. The thing I want to stress, I make the best that I can make. Whether it's a frame or an oil tank.

*What do you feel are the outer limits for rideable bikes in terms of frame dimensions and rake?*

The most radical frame we build for the public has a neck that's raised ten inches and the rake is 45 degrees. I have determined that to be safe. The average guy is six feet tall and he will fit one of those frames. If a frame is stretched more than ten inches most guys can't see over the handle bars.

But sometimes I see a less radical bike with a six-over front end and I can see that the rake and trail is totally lost. I can see that the builder didn't understand or care about how the bike worked. So he set it up that way for the look. Some bikes with a thirty-over front end are safer than a shorter bike because they are set up correctly. Builders must consider the geometry.

*What do you like to see people run for trail?*

We have a diagram that we like to give to people. For normal Harley guys, most of the guys are in the cruising or touring end of it. They want a bike that's more stable. With bigger rear tires you want to get up to about 4 inches of trail.

*What about Jockey shifts, from a safety standpoint, for the average rider?*

I rode them forever. I did take them off my own motorcycles though because I couldn't say this is the way to go for my customers. In my own mind I have a responsibility for the safety of what I build.

When I did build them I had my own way of doing it. I figure the only time you have trouble is in first gear, that's when you have to put your foot down. I set them up so the first 3 inches of pedal movement was the clutch, the last two inches of movement knocked it from first gear to neutral.

*Lots of choppers use chain drive, which means you can put a caliper on the sprocket, How do these work with the chain lube and all the rest?*

I started with a caliper of the chain sprocket in 1977 and ran with only that, no front brakes. Oil is thrown out or off the sprocket by centrifugal force, so it isn't a problem. And those were O-ring chains so the little bit of oil film that you did get on the sprocket would just burn off. We have run belt systems for the past 15 years that also incorporate a brake system into the pulley.

Now I like having disc brakes. I want to stop six inches short of the Cadillac. I used to put 16 inch rotors with multiple calipers on the back. That's total overkill considering you can only match the rubber. That is, if you've got three calipers on the rotor and one skinny tire, what good

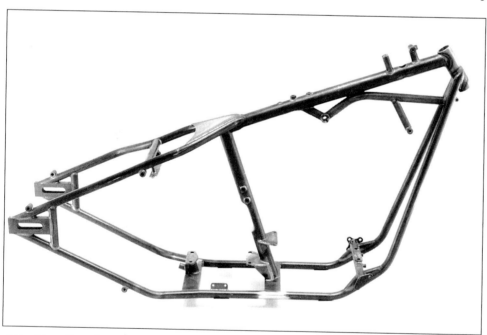

*Like his soft-tail type frame this rigid frame from Pat Kennedy is built from chrome-moly - to better handle the extra stresses imposed on a chopper frame. Accepts most Big Twins with 4 or 5-speed transmission. Available in various dimensions. Kennedy Custom Motorcycles*

do they do? You have too much brake for the tire. Now I run three, eight inch disc brakes; two in front and one in back. The dual eight inch front rotors is a good working, clean looking setup.

The biggest thing on brakes is having the correct caliper to piston to brake line ratio. You have to coordinate on both master and caliper piston(s) size, and the hand strength of the rider. A six foot three biker has more strength in his hand so he gets a bigger master cylinder piston while a small woman doesn't have as much strength so I would give her a smaller diameter master cylinder piston. My levers are somewhat adjustable for that same reason, some people have short fingers and can't reach way out there for the lever.

*Any final comments on building choppers?*

Frame geometry is most important. Centered motors is a biggie. And you have to remember that a lot of the parts people are putting on 120 horsepower bikes were designed for Harleys with 52 horses at the rear wheel. I sell wheels with 80 and more spokes and stainless steel hubs because I was tearing up the 40 spoke wheels with aluminum hubs.

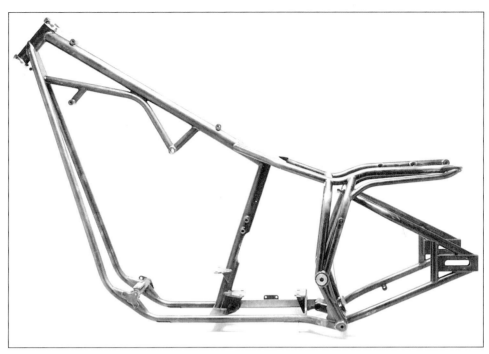

*Weighing in at only 55 pounds with swingarm, this chrome moly frame from Kennedys is available as a Wrangler with 40 degree neck, accepts a 12 over fork assembly. Also available as an Outlaw model with 43 degrees of rake, accepts 20 over fork assembly. Kennedy Custom Motorcycles*

*For Pat Kennedy there is only one type of motorcycle.*

*Chapter Three*

# Chassis Components

## Forks, Brakes and Other Important Stuff

Even if the chopper you build is a hardtail, you still have to equip it with a front fork, thus you will find a discussion of the various fork types just a little farther along. Some choppers have suspension on both ends, so we've included information on soft-tail type shocks as well. And no matter which type of suspension the new bike does or doesn't carry, you need some good brakes to slow the beast down.

*Though they were quite common on the original choppers, girders are hard to find and seldom seen today. This example is part of a Donnie Smith chopper.*

## THE FORK

When it comes to forks for modern choppers, the choice is large and growing. We tend to think all the old choppers used springer forks, but an equal number used hydraulic front ends and there were plenty of girder fork assemblies as well. It might help to take a look at the three main fork types.

## WHAT FITS WHAT

The neck and fork stem bearings are the same on all late model Big Twins, Sportsters and nearly all aftermarket frames. In theory any triple tree should work on any frame. There are, of course, certain exceptions so you need to pay attention to the recommendations of the fork manufacturer.

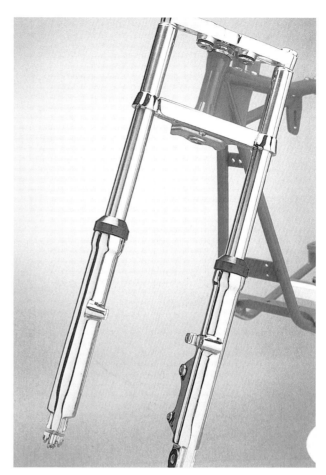

*These 41mm complete fork assemblies come either chrome or polished, ready for single or dual disc brakes, in stock, dimensions, 2 under or 2 to 8 over lengths. CCI*

*Rolling Thunder springers use flush-mount hardware and come in various lengths. Two "models" are available, depending on the frame rake.*

Before you buy a new fork assembly consider that all the components that make up the front end of the bike must be designed (or modified) to work with all the other parts. A wide-style fork will require the right wheel hub and the right brackets or spacers to mount the front fender. Make sure there is some provision for a fork stop, and be sure that any provision for a stop located on the neck matches the provision on the lower triple tree.

When adjusting the fork stops remember that if the bike goes over in the parking lot the force of the fall will likely force the bars past the normal end-of-travel. This means you need more clearance between the bars and the tank than you might think you do.

33

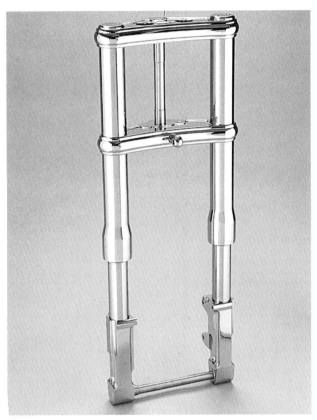

*These inverted forks combine Storz suspension quality with Ness radiused billet trees. Available in two lengths, mid or wide-glide. Ness*

*These zero degree trees carved from billet come in 41 and 39 mm sizes, in mid and wide-glide spacing. Use internal stops on Ness and many factory frames, external stops on all others. Chrome or polished. Ness*

## HYDRAULIC FORKS

A hydraulic, or tube fork, combines the spring and shock in one unit. Hydraulic forks come in wide-glide, narrow-glide, right side up (conventional) and upside down configurations. The terms wide or narrow glide refer to the distance between the two fork tubes. Most factory wide-style forks, for example, measure nearly ten inches center-to-center (exact dimensions vary between the various Harley-Davidson models). Sportsters and many Dynas come with narrow glide forks. In addition the aftermarket offers "mid-glide" forks with tube spacing that's between the narrow and wide dimensions.

Up until recently, most forks used on street-driven V-twins utilized what we might call conventional designs. That is, the tubes, or smaller diameter part of the fork assembly, bolts to the triple clamp. The lower leg, the larger diameter part of the assembly with the caliper mounting lugs, slides up and down on the tubes. The spring that holds up the front of the bike is inside the tube, as is the fork oil. Because of the oil and the damper assembly, the fork is in essence both a spring and a shock absorber.

The most modern of the hydraulic forks are known as inverted, or "upside down." Used for years on competition bikes, this design inverts the two major components. The larger diameter part of the fork is now bolted to the triple clamps. The tubes become the components that move up and down with the front wheel. By clamping the larger diameter member to the triple trees this newer design puts the strongest member in the triple trees - which reduces flex and makes for a more stable front end. This design also reduces unsprung weight by making the smaller diameter part of the fork the part that moves with the wheel over bumps. Most conventional OEM-type forks use damper rods. More sophisticated fork assemblies are "cartridge style."

The two most common tube diameters used in current fork assemblies measure 39mm and 41mm. The 39mm tubes are normally run in a narrow-glide configuration and are used on Sportsters and some Dyna and later FXR models. The 41mm forks come in three basic versions, FLT, Softail Custom and Heritage (also Fat Boy). The FLT tubes are the shortest, with

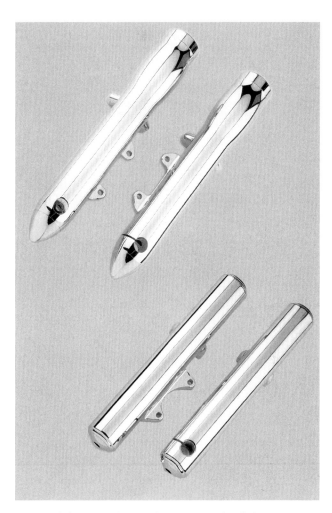

*One of the nice things about a standard 41 or 39mm fork is the variety of lower legs available like these torpedo and smooth examples from Arlen Ness.*

Heritage next in length and Softail Custom being the longest of all. Longer and shorter tubes are available from the aftermarket.

In addition to OEM designs, many of the catalog companies offer their own fork assemblies with or without triple trees. Custom Chrome has a Regency front end while Arlen Ness offers a variety of unique fork assemblies.

When buying extended hydraulic forks it's important to remember that the extra length and rake put a lot of additional stress on the tubes. If they flex they probably aren't working. Some forks are made from extra heavy-wall tubing for this reason.

*New springer forks are as close as your local Custom Chrome dealer. Chrome plated or black and chrome, these come 2 under or up to 6 over.*

# Trail and Raked Trees

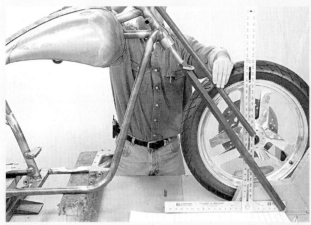

*For demonstration purposes we position the tire where a set of 0-degree trees would place it and check trail.*

*We have about 6 inches of trail, more than is ideal (in hindsight the bike should be sitting at ride height).*

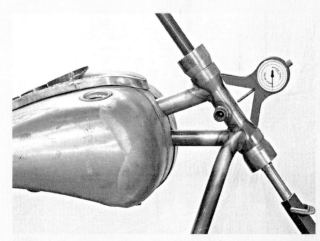

*We need to know the difference between the neck and the fork tube, so start by checking the neck.*

Experienced builders often know that a particular frame and wheel combination will require a tube of a certain length in order to achieve the desired ride height. Many also know what the trail figures are for certain combinations of frame rake, and triple-tree. Most of us reading this book aren't professional bike builders, however. And for that reason I repeat here the comments of Frank Pedersen, a die-hard chopper builder from Olathe, Kansas.

As Frank explains: "If they have a frame with the rear wheel installed, say its a 40 degree Swedish style frame from Chopper Guys. I suggest they set it on blocks at ride height, with the front end a little higher than the rear because it will settle down once it's sitting on the kick stand. You can use conduit, or any long straight tube, to set up a line though the neck and down to the bench, and then mark that pivot point on the bench. Now set the front wheel in place, with some kind of fixture, so the wheel contact patch is four inches (or whatever you want) behind the pivot point. That's your trail. Next, mock up a piece of conduit in place of the actual fork tubes, from the position of the top triple tree to the wheel hub. Use a protractor from the hardware store to figure the difference between the angle of the neck, and the angle of the mocked up fork tube. That is the amount of rake you need in the trees to get the four inches of trail."(Note: be sure the conduit or tube you use can't sag and throw off your figures.)

"For me the ideal trail figure is 3-1/2 to 4-1/2 inches. A Ducati 916 has 3-1/2 inches, while a Softail Custom has 6 inches. The bike I rode to Sturgis this year is a pretty long bike with a 250 tire, that bike has four inches of trail and it works really well.

You can use the same set up described above to figure out the length of the tubes. To quote Frank again, "You have the wheel sitting there, and the conduit mocked up in place of the fork tube. You know where the trees are, so now you can figure the full length of the tube and lower leg. Add one inch to allow for settling of the sus-

# Trail and Raked Trees

pension once it has some weight on it, or a little more if the forks are more vertical because the more vertical they are the more they will settle or compress."

"Let's say you are using lower legs from a Softail Custom. If you have a total length of 43 inches from axle to top of neck you add one inch, for 44 inches all together. Now measure a stock Softail Custom, with the fork extended. If it is 34 inches then you need fork tubes that are ten inches over or ten inches longer than stock."

Note: Some frame manufacturers provide a chart, as to which fork length to use with which of their frames.

*Then we re-position the "tubes" as they would have to be given the wheel's new position. The difference in the angle of the tubes and the angle of the neck is what you need to achieve by installing raked trees. In this case the angle of the tubes is 4 degrees different than the angle of the neck. We did this little demo quick and dirty, you might want to take a little more time mocking up the position of the tubes.*

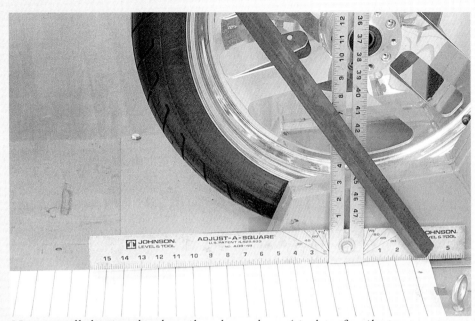

*Now we roll the tire ahead until we have about 4 inches of trail.*

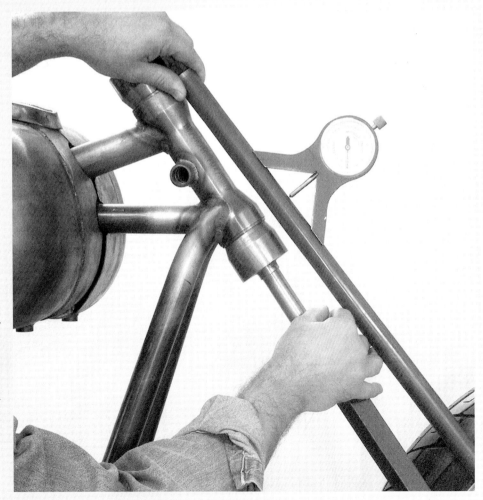

*Built and designed by Donnie Smith, this girder fork assembly will soon find its way into the Chrome Specialties catalogue.*

*When you only have 3 inches (or less) of suspension travel it's important to use high quality components. These rear shocks for soft-tails are adjustable for height. CCI*

## SPRINGER FORKS

Perhaps no one fork style better defines a chopper than the springer. Today there are new springer forks available from a number of companies, including the big company in Milwaukee as well as Paughco in the aftermarket. From Rolling Thunder comes a very smooth springer, available in any length, chrome plated or powder coated (or some interesting combination of the two). Speaking of springers, any new springer should employ a means of controlling the oscillations and harmonics with shocks or some kind of damper.

With a springer fork the triple trees are often integral to the fork assembly, so there's no easy way to adjust the trail, which is why Rolling Thunder offers two versions of their work, one for frames with less than 33 degrees of rake and one for more radical frames with more than 33 degrees of rake. Pat Kennedy ads the comment that,"the length of rocker you use on a springer affects the trail."

Many new springer fork assemblies, like the one from Custom Chrome, use a top tree drilled for conventional risers. A few, like those from Paughco, are available with an earlier-style top tree and accept dog-bone style risers.

Some springers take standard size (factory) axles while others do not. Likewise, some of these retro fork assemblies take stock brakes and sheet metal and some do not. A few allow you to order a caliper at the time you order the fork, so you know the caliper is a good fit.

Among the people who believe you can't

have a chopper without a springer front end are the folks at Rolling Thunder. Fausto from Rolling Thunder explained that in order to get a fork of the right length you have to provide them with the bike's dimensions. "We custom manufacture our forks to any length, the customer needs to tell us the ride height, the size of the front wheel and distance from ground to the bottom of the neck. Then we make the springer to match their bike perfectly."

If you ask Fausto what's the best thing about a springer, he doesn't hesitate with the answer. "They look cool. Ours especially. We cut all the components on CNC equipment, everything is TIG welded and triple plated chrome (though powder coating is available as well). The bolts are all polished stainless, flush mounted for a totally smooth look." People need to tell us if the frame has more or less than 33 degrees of rake," explains Fausto, "so we can ship them the right fork assembly."

## GIRDER FORKS

The aptly named girder fork is really nothing more than two "girders" supported by a spring and parallelogram linkage. In the case of the new fork from Donnie Smith the spring is

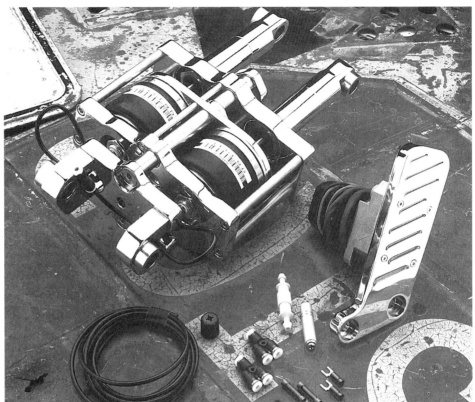

*Have our cake and eat it too. With these air shocks from Legend you can park it in the weeds for that killer stance and then pump it up for a ride down a bumpy road. Ness*

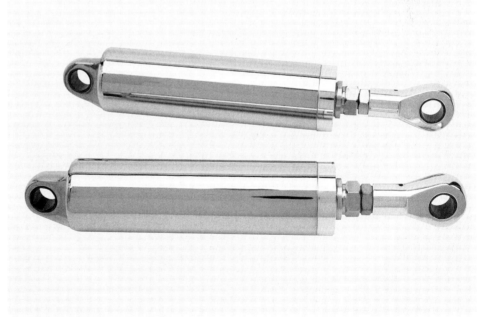

*These shocks from Works allow you to lower the back of the bike up to 1-1/2 inches. Aluminum bodies help the shocks to dissipate heat. Ness*

actually a coil-over that combines a spring and shock into one unit, complete with a collar to adjust the spring pre-load.

## SHOCK ABSORBERS

Like the front fork, the shocks used on most motorcycles combine shocks and springs into one unit. It's easier to understand how each works by looking at the components separately.

If you compress a spring and let go, it doesn't just bounce back to its original position but rather goes well past that point and through a series of diminishing oscillations. In order to dampen those oscillations a shock absorber (technically these are dampers not shocks) is used, generally incorporated into the spring assembly.

The damping is provided by fluid friction, which can create heat. Some inexpensive shocks allow air to mix with the oil, and the oil itself to change viscosity due to the heat. The net result is poor and inconsistent damping.

Quality shock absorbers avoid these problems with components that are larger and built to higher standards. Valves used to control the damping are much more sophisticated to better handle a variety of road conditions and riding styles and the amount of oil is increased. The body of the shock can be made of aluminum to help it run cool. To prevent aeration of the oil, the shock is gas-charged or filled with a premium oil that won't change viscosity.

We are only considering soft-tail type rear suspensions here (and ignore hybrid designs from Gambler and Kosman). When you ride over a bump the shocks of the soft-tail type suspension extend, they don't compress. For this reason the rear suspension needs an external "bump stop." You don't want to make the shocks do the job of limiting suspension travel on compression. Without the additional stop a stiff bump can damage those expensive new shock absorbers.

Before buying shocks you need to

*The small two-piston calipers are a good fit on many springers. The correct bracket and linkage for use with a 10 inch rotor can be ordered for many brands of springer forks. PM*

realize that not all soft-tail type chassis are the same. Even prior to the introduction of the new TC Softails in 2000, the factory used two different shocks, one for the early, 1984 to 1988 bikes, and another that covers bikes built from 1989 to the introduction of the new 2000 models. Most aftermarket frames use the later shocks that fit 1989 to 1999 bikes, but it's always best to ask the frame manufacturer for a recommendation. If you mis-match the frame and shocks damage to the shocks can result.

## AIR SHOCKS

For those who want their bike down in the weeds without the harsh ride that results when you lower a bike to the point where there is no suspension travel left, Legend offers their air shock kit. Similar to units used for some time by the custom car and hot rod builders, these kits consist of two air-shock units that take the place of regular soft-tail type shocks, connected to a small on-board compressor and control unit through small-diameter air lines.

With air shocks you can let the air out when you park the bike for that killer stance, then pump it up again when running down the road. If you add a passenger, just add a little more air pressure at the same time. Air bags actually make a near-perfect spring in the sense that the spring-rate becomes progressively stiffer as the suspension unit is compressed.

Downsides include the added complexity of pumps and gauges, and the fact that the whole kit costs considerably more than standard set of high quality shocks.

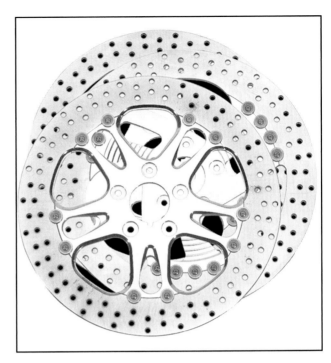

*These "Image" rotors are designed to match the style of various billet wheels and come in 11.5 and 13 inch diameters with outer rotor made from cast ductile iron or stainless. PM*

*With a flash coat of chrome, these ductile iron rotors from GMA offer good looks and a surface that the brake pads can easily grab onto. Biker's Choice*

# Let It Bleed

Anytime the hydraulic system is opened up on either end of the bike you will be forced to bleed the brakes. Hydraulic brake systems work because a fluid cannot be compressed to a smaller volume – though the same cannot be said about air. If there's any air in the system the squeeze on the master cylinder lever will only compress that air, instead of creating useful hydraulic pressure.

In the case of the old Chevy in the garage, the normal bleeding procedure (the most common one anyway) is to fill the master cylinder with fluid, install the cap and have a helper pump the mushy brake pedal. Then while they hold the pedal to the floor you open the bleeder screw. Each time the bleeder screw is opened a little spurt of air and brake fluid escapes. The trick is to close the bleeder *before* the helper lets the pedal pop up.

By doing this repeatedly fresh brake fluid is forced from the master cylinder to the caliper and eventually out the bleeder screw. Any air is pushed out of the bleeder ahead of the fluid. The project is done when the pedal is rock-hard, and fresh brake fluid with no sign of air comes out the bleeder each time it is opened. If, during all this pumping and bleeding, the pedal (or lever) is allowed to snap back while the bleeder is still open air is pulled back *into*

*At Kokesh MC they like to use a brake pump that sucks the fluid through the lines to the bleeder valve. Container prevents brake fluid from filling the pump.*

the caliper.

Though you can follow the same methods for bleeding the brakes on your chopper it doesn't always work. The biggest problem is the small size of the master cylinder piston. There simply isn't much fluid displaced on each stroke. As my mechanic-friend Patrick explains, "With the little master cylinder it takes a long time to move that bubble of air from the master cylinder to the bleeder."

Motorcycles have a couple of additional problems. One is best stated by Elmer, long-time mechanic at Kokesh MC in Spring Lake Park, Minnesota. "If the shape of the handle bars has the master cylinder pointing uphill, then you get a bubble of air in the line right where it connects to the master cylinder. That's the highest point in the system so it's almost impossible to get rid of that bubble. You have to lean the bike over so the master points downhill, or take the master cylinder off the bars and point it downhill.

The other problem is the way aftermarket calipers sometimes mount with the bleeder screw at the bottom. Air always rises so with the bleeder at the bottom you can't really bleed the caliper. The solution is to take the caliper off the bracket and hold it so the bleeder is on top. Then put something between the pads and then get on with the bleeding.

Though this all sounds simple enough more than one intrepid motorcycle mechanic has failed to get all the air out of the brake system. A variety of devices are sold to make the job easier. Some, like the EZ-Bleeder, force fluid in at the bleeder and then through the line to the master cylinder until the reservoir is full and the system is purged of air. The mechanics we spoke with, including Elmer at Kokesh, prefer bleeding machines that attach to the bleeder and then suck the fluid from the reservoir to and through the bleeder.

If you've never bled brakes before you might want to stop at the local shop and buy one of the bleeding devices they sell. Some bikes are just hard to bleed. You have to take it to the shop and let them do it with something like a power bleeder.

No matter how you bleed the brakes, do not settle for a spongy pedal. And be sure to inspect all the junctions for leaks with the system under pressure. Finally, remember non-silicone fluid eats paint.

## BRAKES

Brakes are heat machines. When you squeeze the lever the brake pads are forced against the spinning rotor. The bike slows (hopefully) and the by-product is heat. You've converted moving (or kinetic) energy to heat energy – you can't create or destroy energy, only convert it from one form to another. More physics: a bike traveling 60 miles per hour has four times (not two) the kinetic energy of the same machine at 30 miles per hour.

Some of the old choppers were built without a front brake. All part of the "chopping" or simplifying the bike. Many riders of the period said that "there's so much of the weight on the back of the bike that it really doesn't matter."

But the times change. Jim Morrison is dead, they only play Beatles songs on the Oldies station, and motorcycles need brakes on both ends. Even with allowances for weight distribution, you still have to consider the weight *transfer* that occurs when you hit the brakes. And unless you're really going the extra mile for effect, a disc brake is a much better deal than a drum brake. Disc brakes are self cleaning and offer more brake potential for a given amount of weight. Some of the tiny brake rotors and Mickey Mouse calipers used on the front of the old original choppers weren't much more than window dressing. When the rotor gets too small the caliper doesn't have any leverage to slow the wheel.

If you ask a brake technician for advice regarding the brakes for that new motorcycle, most will simply say that 'more is better.' When the motorcycle is a chopper though, the discussion seems to change. Suddenly the brakes, especially the front brake, becomes less important, often taking a back seat to aesthetics. People cite the old argument that a chopper carries more of its weight on the back tire, so the front brake is less important than on a "regular" motorcycle.

To separate fact from fiction we spoke with Richard, chopper rider and technician at Performance Machine.

"You always need a front brake," says Richard. "You want as much as you can, why go half way. I have a chopper, no way would I fathom taking off the front caliper. A lot of people want to clean up the front wheel, they don't want the visual of seeing a rotor on the front wheel or a master cylinder on the handle bars. They don't want to see a line running from the bars down to the caliper, and they justify it by saying the weight is all on the back wheel, but what about weight transfer. And hey, if I'm in a panic-stop situation I want all the help I can get."

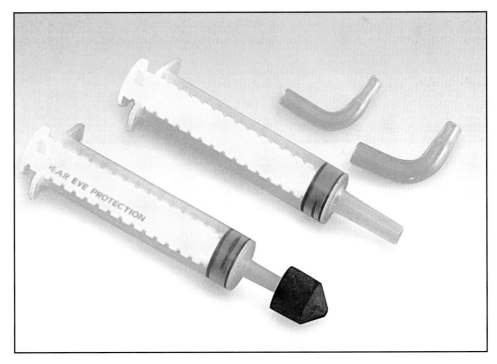

*The EZE Bleeder makes bleeding easier by forcing brake fluid in at the bleeder and filling the system from there to the reservoir. Biker's Choice*

For builders planning to put some brakes on the front wheel Richard suggests that the best brakes depend to a large extent on the fork assembly. "If the bike is a custom rigid with a springer fork, I recommend a dual disc set up with two of our two-piston calipers. Those are nice small calipers, kind of petite, yet they still provide good braking. Which rotor they use will depend on the style of bike and the design of the hub. Some

*Brake pads come in more than one flavor - depending on the rotor surface and your personal tastes.*

*Brake calipers come with two (not shown) four and six pistons. Most are available with integral brackets. Remember to use recommended hardware to attach the calipers to the fork leg or swingarm. PM*

want a simple stainless rotor while others choose high performance full-floating rotors.

"If the front end is hydraulic, a conventional fork, then one or two of our direct bolt-on calipers is probably the best answer. The differential bore four-piston caliper could work here. When they use a tall 21 inch front wheel it gives the bike that long slender look and a six piston caliper might look really good in that application."

If you ask Richard about the likelihood of locking the front wheel on a hard stop, he explains that the potential problem is probably exaggerated. "A well set up front end matched to a sell set up front brake system will always give a rider plenty of feedback and the likelihood of locking the wheel is no different than with a traditional bike."

### ROTOR MATERIALS

Brake rotors can and are manufactured from stainless steel, cast iron, even ductile iron. Cast and ductile iron offer a better coefficient of friction – a surface the pad can more easily grab onto. Cast iron rotors are now available from both GMA and Performance Machine with a flashing of chrome nickel to improve the aesthetics. Note, this is not the same as chrome plating a rotor, which generally leaves the surface warped, and so slippery that the pad can't get any kind of grip to slow down the bike.

Given the fact that these are choppers, most riders will opt for stainless steel. Formed by adding chrome to cast iron, stainless rotors are super hard and will virtually never wear out. The hardness makes it more difficult though for the pad to grab hold of the rotor.

Brake pads too are manufactured from various materials. Organic pads, this includes Kevlar, are softer and better suited to use against the softer cast and ductile iron materials. The other major type of pad, sintered iron, is better used in combination with stainless steel rotors. The important thing is to get a good match between the rotor and pad material so you get good braking without damage to the rotor. Lingering questions regarding pad and rotor combinations can be best answered by the technicians employed by all of the manufacturers.

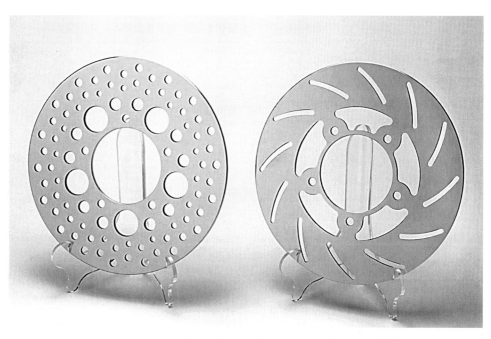

*Stainless steel rotors are often available in various designs to better match your wheels. Ness*

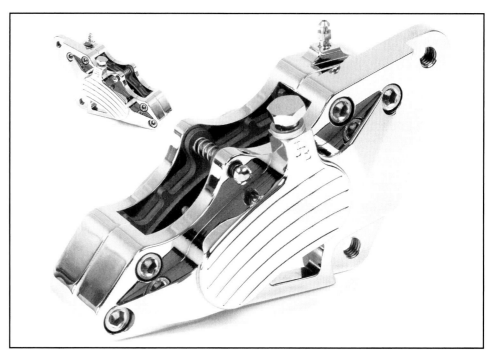

*These JayBrake four piston progressive calipers come with integral brackets and all necessary hardware for mounting to most bikes. Biker's Choice*

45

# Hydraulic Ratios

A demonstration of hydraulic ratios might help explain the importance of correctly matching the master cylinder and the caliper(s). The pressure of the hydraulic fluid at the master cylinder outlet is determined by that old formula from physics class: Pressure = Force/Area. So if you put ten pounds of force on a master cylinder piston with one square inch of area, you have created a pressure of 10psi. If you change the master cylinder to a design with only 1/2 square inch of piston area, then you've created twice the pressure.

Assuming 10 psi of pressure in the lines and a caliper with one square inch of piston area, the force on the brake pad will be 10 pounds (Force = Pressure X Area). If you double the piston area you also double the force on the brake pad. Thus the way to achieve maximum force on the brake pads is with a small master cylinder piston working multiple caliper pistons with relatively high total area. For everything you gain, however, you likewise give something up. Small master cylinder pistons don't displace much liquid, and may not provide enough lever travel to fully extend the caliper pistons.

In the real world, brake manufacturers and salespeople skip the computer program and simply rely on certain "rules of thumb" to correctly match the master cylinder with the caliper(s).

Bill Gardner offers the following guidelines: With a single new caliper, 2 or 4 piston design, on the rear or front, use a master cylinder with a 5/8inch bore. If you have dual calipers on the front, whether they're 4 or 6-piston calipers, use a master cylinder with a 3/4 inch piston bore. If in doubt, ask the sales person or manufacturer of your new brake components for a recommendation.

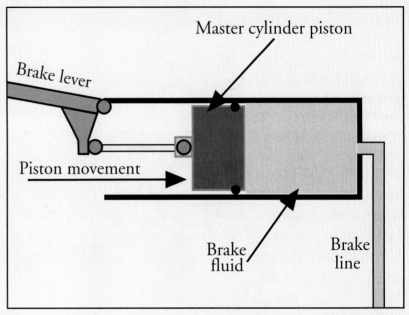

*The bigger the master cylinder piston the more fluid is displaced. As piston size grows however the amount of pressure (all other things being equal) goes down. Output pressure is also affected by the lever ratio, which is why some hi-end and metric OEM masters have adjustable pivots.*

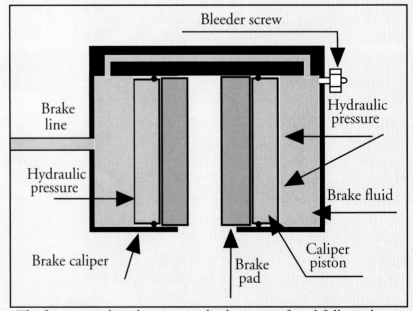

*The force created in the master cylinder is transferred fully to the caliper pistons. The more piston area the more net force is created by a certain pressure. The trade off: more pistons (or calipers) require more volume to move all those pistons. The trick, as always, is to find that balance point.*

## MATCH MAKING

You also need to match the size of the master cylinder bore to the caliper(s). Essentially, a smaller diameter master cylinder piston creates more hydraulic pressure but displaces less fluid, than a larger diameter piston (all other things being equal). But before getting too deep into hydraulic ratios it might be helpful to discuss the laws that govern hydraulics. Specifically, you need to keep in mind two facts:

1) Pressure in the brake system is equal over all surfaces of the system.

2) A fluid cannot be compressed to a smaller volume.

## THE FLUID

Brake fluid is a very specialized hydraulic fluid, designed to operate in a very dirty environment and withstand very high temperatures without boiling. When a liquid boils it becomes a gas, a compressible material, sensed by the rider as a very soft or spongy brake lever or pedal. Quality brake fluid will remain viscous at nearly any temperature and resist boiling up to 400 degrees Fahrenheit.

There are three grades of brake fluid commonly available: DOT 3, DOT

*The right side view of these wheels is enhanced through the use of a left side front rotor and small rear rotor. PM*

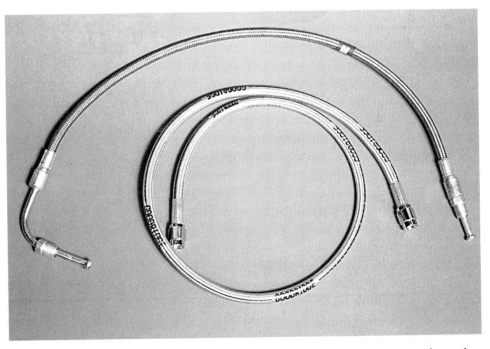

*What we call stainless brake lines come in various forms and sizes. Some have the proper ends already attached as an integral part of the line while others have a female fitting to which you can attach the right flare or banjo fitting.*

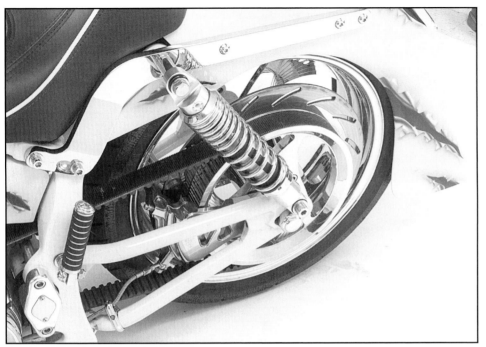

*To clean up the back of the bike and open up the right side of the wheel you can combine the belt pulley with the rear brake rotor and caliper. Ness*

*Available 9 inches wide, in 16 or 18 inch diameters, these cast wheels feature one hell of an offset for a very unique appearance. Drive side pulley and brake caliper combination are available as well. Ness*

4 and DOT 5. DOT 3 and 4 are glycol-based fluids with dry boiling points of 401 and 446 degrees Fahrenheit respectively. Though DOT 3 and 4 fluids are often used in automobiles, you might not want to use them in your motorcycle for two reasons: first, they absorb water from the environment; second, they attack most paints.

When compared to the DOT 3 and 4 brake fluids, DOT 5 brake fluid shows some distinct advantages. DOT 5 fluid is silicone based, meaning a higher boiling point (500 degrees Fahrenheit, dry), no tendency to absorb water and no reaction when spilled on a painted surface. It costs more and is reputed to be slightly compressible, though street riders never seem to notice any difference in "feel" after switching to silicone fluid.

New Harley-Davidsons have used silicone-based fluid since the early 1980s and the fluid you will find on the shelf of the dealership or quality aftermarket shop is probably DOT 5, silicone-based fluid. No matter which fluid you decide to use, stick with that fluid. You should never mix the two types of fluid.

The brake fluid is not compressible which means the pressure at the master cylinder outlet is applied fully to the pistons in the calipers. None of that pressure is "used up" compressing the fluid between the master cylinder and the calipers. This also means that the pressure at the master cylinder outlet is the same pressure that is applied to all the surfaces in the brake system.

When you buy a master cylinder and

calipers for the front of that new soft-tail style machine, you not only need to buy the components that best match your intended use and budget, you also need to buy components that are correctly matched to each other.

## FINAL NOTES

When you install those new calipers on the fork or swingarm be sure to center the caliper over the rotor (shims are usually provided for this purpose) and use the correct mounting brackets and bolts. The mounting bolts must be very high quality because the full force of a panic stop is transmitted from the caliper to the chassis through the bracket and bolts. Use bolts that came with the caliper kit or those that are recommended by the manufacturer.

Most aftermarket calipers come in a variety of finishes, including satin, polished and chrome plate. Though it's a small thing, try to buy a chrome caliper if the lower legs and wheel are chrome plated.

Keep all the components matched: the right master cylinder matched to the right calipers to produce the correct pressure and travel at the lever, the right pads matched to the right rotor surface. Keep everything neat and allow no dirt or impurities into the hydraulic part of the system.

The biggest problem most people have with the installation of the brakes comes down to bleeding. They don't get all the air out of the system and the lever or pedal is spongy as a result. For help in that regard we've provided a side-bar on bleeding brakes. If you're still having trouble, swallow your pride and take it to a good shop and let them do the bleeding.

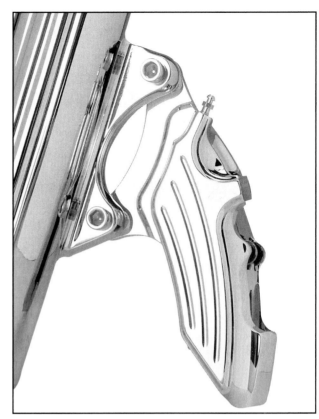

*These six piston calipers come in chrome or polish and feature integral brackets with very sleek styling. Ness*

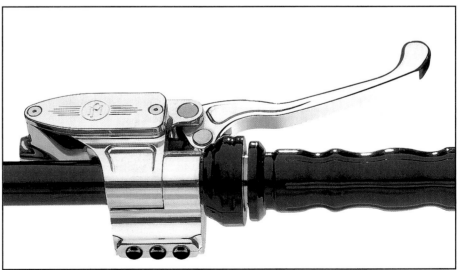

*Most front master cylinders come in 5/8, 11/16 and 3/4 inch bores for single and dual caliper applications. Check with the brake manufacturer or rep for a recommendation. PM*

## Chapter Four

# Wheels and Tires

## Lighter, Taller, Wider

The wheels and tires you put on your bike have as much to do with the final look of the machine as anything else. In both a visual and functional sense, the importance of the wheels can't be overstated. Though there is certainly a functional aspect

to wheels, when it comes to choppers the visuals are the single most important thing most of us consider.

**WHEEL TYPES**

What many of us simply call "billet" wheels are

*The wheels are probably the second most important thing you choose for the bike, after the frame. They affect the way the bike looks, rides and handles, and have impact on your choice of brakes and other drivetrain components as well. PM*

actually two or three different types of aluminum wheels. True billet wheels are carved from a billet (or a solid chunk) of aluminum. Most billet wheels are manufactured from 6061 T6, the first four digits identify the alloy while the T6 number refers to the heat treating specification.

Cast is the other major type of aluminum wheel. The alloy in this case is generally 356 aluminum. The expense of buying forged billets of aluminum is eliminated through casting, though tooling costs are considerable. Most cast wheels have a rim that is an integral part of the assembly instead of being a separate piece bolted or welded to the spokes. Because there may be some porosity in the cast material, chrome plating is more difficult with a cast wheel.

At one time the billet wheels used spokes (or a center section) cut from forged aluminum, bolted or welded to a separate rim assembly. Currently there are at least two methods of manufacturing a true billet wheel with an integral rim.

With "split and spin" a large round disc of billet aluminum is set into a special lathe or fixture. The fixture spins the raw disc of aluminum while a bit comes in at the edge of the spinning billet and carefully splits the aluminum at the edge. By carefully splitting and

*These forged aluminum wheels feature softer edges for a look similar to a cast wheel. Patterned after the 12 spoke American mag, the 12 spoke would be ideal for certain high performance go-fast hardtails. PM*

*With a new look all their own, these cast wheels feature a huge offset and are wide enough for 250 rubber. Ness*

rolling this edge, two rim halves are formed at the edge of the spinning aluminum billet. After the rim is formed the incomplete wheel is moved through a series of CNC lathes and mills where the spokes are fashioned.

A one-piece billet wheel with an integral rim can also be created in a forging operation. In this case a rather large disc of billet aluminum is forged between a pair of dies. The extremely high pressure gradually molds the aluminum disc into a shape resembling a wheel with a crude rim at the outer edge. After the dies have "forged" the disc into this basic shape, the rough wheel is machined to the final shape.

The forging operation creates some advantages, it makes for very dense aluminum that polishes easily, and it creates a strong radial grain pattern.

All this talk of aluminum wheels may be moot however. This is a chopper book, and what choppers need – besides a Panhead engine and Sportster tank – is two wheels laced with wire.

## WIRE WHEELS

The wire wheels offered for sale today come in 40, 80, 120 and 240 spokes with rims of aluminum or steel. Diameters include 15, 16, 17, 18, 19 and 21 inches. Widths start at about two inches for skinny 21 inch front rims and go to at least nine inches for 15 and 16 and 18 inch rear wheels. Spokes come in steel or stainless steel, in round, square and twisted configurations. The most common spokes used today are 6/8 gauge, though heavier gauges are available. Not all spokes are the same in terms of quality either. The best spokes come with well-known brand names, including one of the best known brand names in the world - Harley-Davidson.

At the center of the wheel is the hub, available in steel or aluminum. Not all hubs use the same spoke indexing pattern, the Motor Company has used at least 3 different indexing patterns over the years including one that started in 1997. In addition, not all spokes fit all hubs. The hub must match the bike, i.e. wide or narrow-style fork and single or double-disc brakes. The hub manufacturer will suggest spokes, some are quite specific as to which spokes must be used with which hubs.

When discussing spokes the name Buchanan comes to mind. This maker of polished stainless spokes does the manufacturing in the US, the spokes are available in various shapes including conventional round spokes as well as twisted-rectangular designs. Buchanans can also lace up almost any imaginable rim and hub combination for those hard to find, or hard to fit, situations

When it comes to rims, the names Excel and Sun come to mind, both manufacturers of high quality aluminum rims. Available either as rims or as part of a wheel assembly, sizes range from skinny 21 inch wheels to relatively wide 16 and 18 inch rims meant for the rear of that fat-tired

*Most of the new billet wheels are available in either polished or chrome plated finish. On the left the Player, while on the right is the Vintage. PM*

two-wheeled hot rod.

There are also some very nice rims manufactured from chrome plated steel. These come raw or already assembled in any size you can imagine. Arlen Ness offers his own "Fat 40" wheels made up of their own chrome plated rim and radius design hub, laced with fat, heavy-duty spokes. Landmark and American Wire Wheel offer 80 and 100 spoke wheel assemblies with straight or twisted spokes and chrome plated hubs and steel rims. Some of these can even be run tubeless, as the area where the spokes come through the rim has been sealed with an epoxy-type material.

Custom Chrome has some very nice wheels assembled from chrome plated steel hubs matched up to stainless steel rims. These 40 spoke wheels come in a variety of 15 and 16 inch sizes. We should also mention that not all rims are laced up in a traditional criss-cross pattern. Also available are the radial spoked wheels, where the spokes simply radiate out from the hub to the rim. Most of these either use more than 40 spokes or very large, heavy duty "spokes" measuring 3/8 inch or more in diameter.

Before deciding which style of spoked wheel to buy, consider that conventional spoked wheels get their torsional strength from the fact that the spokes criss-cross and do not run straight out from the hub to the rim. Forces or acceleration or deceleration are absorbed by spokes under tension. Radial spoke designs give up that design advantage though most use 80 or more spokes, or spokes that are much larger than the typical 6/8 gauge.

In the end, if you can't find the wheel you're looking for, you aren't looking hard enough. They're all here, from simple 40 spoke rims with chrome plated steel

rims, to fancy 220 and 240 spoke designs. Consider all the criteria before buying wheels. That includes cost, weight and the wheel's ability to handle the expected braking and acceleration loads.

## PUT TOGETHER YOUR OWN

You don't have to buy an already assembled spoked wheel assembly. Hubs, rims and spokes can be purchased separately and screwed together to create your own unique wheel, or a wheel with a certain amount of built-in off-set. Though lacing up a hub and rim isn't exactly rocket science, it is a job that requires a certain amount of experience particularly when it comes to the truing. In short, if you can't find what you want already assembled, this is one job better left to professionals.

## TIRES

First, the technical stuff. All tires have an epistle written on the sidewall though few of us take the time to do any quality reading. Here's what all those letters and numbers really mean.

Let's look at a Avon 160/70 VR 17 73V TL AV281. The first numbers give the approximate section width of the tire in millimeters. The width of the tire through a section just outside the rim

*These Fat 40 wheels utilize oversize spokes for strength and a radius billet hub for good looks. Complete assembly is chrome plated, comes with bearings and spacers. Available in various widths, and 16, 18 and 21 inch diameters. Ness*

*Hubs, whether aluminum or steel, need to be matched to the correct spokes and rim. These radius hubs are from Arlen Ness.*

*You can put the polish away, these Excel alloy rims are chrome plated and come in 21X1.85 to 16X5.5 inches. Ness*

*These stainless steel spokes come in round, radius and diamond and are designed specifically for Arlen Ness or Performance Machine hubs.*

and not the width of the tire at its widest point. The second number describes the profile. The number 70 means the tire is 70 percent as tall as it is wide. A 40 would represent a very low-profile tire, one that is only 40 percent as tall as it is wide. The number, seventeen, represents the applicable tire diameter. V is the speed rating, R indicates radial construction, 73V is the load index, a numerical code associated with the maximum load a tire can carry at the speed indicated by the speed symbol.

In the example above, V is the speed symbol, the maximum speed at which the tire can carry a load corresponding to its load index. The TL means the tire is tubeless and must be mounted on a tubeless-type rim. The AV281 is the model specific identification code.

## THE SPEED RATINGS

All tires carry a speed rating. These ratings start at S, good up to 112 miles per hour; H, good up to 130 miles per hour; V, good up to 150 miles per hour and W, good up to 169 miles per hour. Looking through the Avon chart again, tires rated VB and VR can be run at speeds up to 210 kilometers per hour (roughly 131 miles per hour), the ZR can operate at speeds up to 150 miles per hour while the V300 is good to 186 miles per hour, faster than most of us will ever ride a motorcycle, much less a chopper.

We should talk a little about the profile of the tire we put on the rear of our new chopper. The 250/40X18 from Avon uses a very short sidewall, while the 230/60X15 uses a much taller sidewall. A few points about these two tires, especially in light of the types of bikes being discussed here.

First, the look of the two tires is very different. The 230 has a more traditional profile while the 250 looks more modern, like something you might find on a new Corvette or lowered Toyota. Second, the two tires have nearly the same diameter. To quote Craig Knapp from Hoppe and Associates, the sales, technical and marketing office for Avon, "We designed the 250 to have about the same overall diameter as the 230, that way it fits current frames, fenders and swingarms."

Craig adds, "To clarify the 230/250 further,

the 230's taller sidewall and stiffer bias-construction can allow for lower air pressures to soften the ride when used on a hardtail. However, this practice can exaggerate the squared-off feel and handling characteristics the 230 exhibits when compared to a higher-crowned tire like the 250.

Despite its width, the 250 has the more rounded contour – and in most cases will provide an easier and lighter cornering feel. With the 250 being of radial construction, its low sidewall height makes using low air pressures a somewhat risky proposition over rough roads! Since this tire has no O.E. fitment, it falls into a purely custom application category and though a radial front would be the obvious choice, no specific recommendations are given as to selection of fronts."

Just a few more points to make with regard to tires: Front and rear tires have different shapes and should be kept on their respective ends of the motorcycle. The tire data book mentioned earlier is available from all the manufacturers and will provide information as to the recommended rim width for a certain tire, the overall diameter and circumference of the tire as well as the maximum load. Automotive and motorcycle rims adhere to slightly different specifications, meaning an automotive tire used on a motorcycle rim might not center correctly resulting in a very lumpy ride. Automotive tires also have those square shoulders which makes turn-in challenging at best. Finally, most 17 inch tires are meant for the sport bike market and are of a smaller total diameter than the 15, 16 and 18 inch tires mentioned above. Meaning they may not fit typical V-twin frames, fenders and gearing scenarios as well as the tires meant for this market.

*Though the 250 Avon shown is an 18 inch tire, the actual diameter is about the same as a 230X15. CCI*

*Though they're stylish, Pat Kennedy makes 120 and 240 spoke wheels and components primarily because they are very, very strong. Available in all the popular sizes, including rear rims up to 8.5 inches wide. Kennedy's Custom MC*

## Chapter Five

# Engine Options

## From Twin Cams to Knuckles

Along with the style of frame you're going to choose for the new chopper, you also have to consider which type of engine you want to get this new beast down the road. Options include the tried and true Evo-style engine from Milwaukee or the aftermarket, and the newer Twin Cam from Harley-Davidson, available with or without the counter-balancers (the B version). Many hard-tail and soft-tail style chassis bolt the engine solid to the frame. If the

*Weber dual throat carburetors are available in various configurations, including this very chopperesque downdraft setup. Webers allow jet changes while the carb is on the bike and venturi changes as well. Can be equipped with velocity stacks or air cleaner as shown. CCI*

engine is a TC 88B with counter-balancers, then that isn't a problem. If however, the engine is a 113 cubic inch aftermarket mill, then you have to understand that the engine will shake, and that those vibes will be transmitted directly to your body.

Part of choosing an engine comes down to style. Retro rides need a new-old engine. Maybe one of the new Panheads or even a Knucklehead. Modern interpretations of the chopper theme might be better off with a four inch bore Evo from TP Engineering, or a Twin Cam B from the local Harley-Davidson dealer.

*Twin Cam engines are available complete from your local dealer with or without counterbalancers. Can be purchased in aluminum or black and chrome.*

## TWIN CAM

For all those riders who want to power their new bike with the latest offering from Milwaukee, complete TC 88 engines are available from your local dealer, in both B and non-B form. George from Delano Harley-Davidson, reports the following retail prices:

The 88B in black and chrome, $4995, in aluminum the same engine is $3995. A matching transmission is $1569 in black and silver and only $1395 in basic aluminum. The non-B TC engine (a Dyna engine) sells for $4495.

Many of the frame manufacturers offer their most popular chassis in var-

*The TC 88B must be used with the matching transmission, as shown, though the non-B engine can be adapted to a Evo frame and used with a standard soft-tail style transmission.*

*Your TC can be bumped to 116 cubes with this kit from Jim's.*

ious configurations to match the engine of your choice. American Thunder, for example, states that all their frames, "Can be ordered for Twin Cam A or B." Because the Twin Cam engines interlock with the transmission, there is no conventional boss on the back of the engine, like on an Evo, to bolt the back of the engine to the frame. That doesn't mean a Twin Cam A motor can't be installed into a frame designed for an Evo.

To install an A motor into an Evo frame it's necessary to simply install an adapter on the back of the motor. This provides the necessary mounting points. There may be a slight clearance problem between the new adapter and the frame's center post, nothing that can't be resolved through the judicious use of a four-inch grinder.

The A motor installed in such a fashion into an Evo frame can then be matched up to a five or six-speed pre-2000 soft-tail style transmission. Essentially you have an Evo-style drive train in an Evo frame with a TC motor for power.

The B motor can't be easily adapted to an Evo Frame, however. First, there's the problem of the welded-in center post, which is deleted from the new factory Softail frames, and similar frames from the aftermarket. Then there's the front motor mount. What separates a B motor from an A motor is the counterbalancers and drive system. This means the cases and front motor mount had to be changed to make room for the weights and the chain drive. The front motor mount is more like a tube that hangs on an "axle" that runs from one side of the

*If you're looking to increase the displacement of a TC without installing fly-wheels, S&S offers this 100 inch kit, includes pistons, cylinders, heads, carb cam and hardware.*

frame to the other. What all this means is that Twin Cam B engines need to be used as a unit with the matching transmission – and then installed into a chassis designed for the B engine.

Now that the Twin Cam engines have been out for awhile, there is no shortage of parts from both Screamin' Eagle and the aftermarket to make the newer motor howl. For more displacement there are the well known 95 inch kits from SE, and similar big-bore kits from the aftermarket. Additional increases in displacement can be had through the installation of a stroker kit. By increasing the stock 3-3/4 inch bore to 4 inches, and the stock 4 inch stroke to 4-5/8 inches, the displacement can be boosted to 116 cubic inches with kits from companies like Jim's, S&S or Zipper's. There are also hop up kits from Head Quarters and others that retain the stock dis-placement, boosting power through the use of ported heads and new camshafts.

## EVO

The Evo engine is a tried and true mill. Before you call this engine an old timer, consider the aftermarket designs from S&S, TP Engineering and Merch to name only three. All offer cylinders that measure four inches or more, which can be mated to 4, 4-1/4, or 4-1/2 inch flywheel assemblies. Buying or building an engine with 125 horsepower is no longer a difficult thing to do. TP Engineering has a 121 cubic inch V-Twin based on a 4-1/8 inch cylinders while Zipper's offers a 114 cubic inch engine based on 4-1/4 inch cylinders mated to 4 inch 'wheels, or a 131 cubic inch monster motor assembled using 4-1/4 inch cylinders and a 4-5/8 inch flywheel assembly. Granted, the average chopper is pretty heavy, what with the big fairing and the stereo and that massive front fender. Even so, 120 cubic inches ought to be enough for just about any rider.

A discussion of the Evo must include the original 80 inch example from Milwaukee. With all the lights and cameras focused on the big block examples from the aftermar-

*An innovator in the industry, engines from TP engineering feature oversize pinion shafts and countersunk case bolts. Buy a 107 or 113 based on a 4 inch bore, or a 121 with a 4-1/8 inch bore. TP*

ket, it's easy to forget what a good, and durable engine the original Evo is. In what's commonly called "hot rod 80" form these engines put out an easy 80 horsepower and 80 foot pounds of torque, with plenty of that power available relatively low in the RPM range where most of us ride. With more compression and camshaft these engines can be nudged close to 100 horses, though there is some trade off in low end grunt. For a chopper that's plenty of horsepower for most riders.

Harley-Davidson dealers can still order new Evo engines from the factory, and many have one or two examples in stock. List prices are $3995 in black and chrome and $2995 in aluminum. These engines come with a warranty but ship without the carb or alternator. These are list prices, there seems to be some discounting going on out there.

Because a number of riders are replacing 80 inch Evos with much bigger aftermarket engines there are some really good deals to be had on complete used Evos. Before snapping up that great deal, remember that the motor isn't any good unless it's legal. The laws vary state by state (see Title Considerations in Chapter Two), but it's not a good idea to buy any engine unless you have an MSO, or proof of legal ownership, that will satisfy the authorities in your state.

## SHOVELHEAD

Introduced in 1966, the first Shovelheads were really just a Panhead with a new top end. That is, they used the same generator bottom end as the preceding Panhead. Until 1970 that is, when the Shovel heads and cylinders were grafted onto the "new" alternator bottom end.

*Among the complete engines on the market are these units from RevTech which come in 88 and 100 cubic inch displacements. All engines are built for RevTech in a ISO 9000 facility. CCI*

There are plenty of old Shovelhead engines for sale out there. Before buying a motor that may need to be rebuilt and comes complete with issues surrounding the legal paperwork, why not just belly up to the bar and buy a complete new alternator-style Shovelhead.

S&S sells complete Shovelhead engines in displacements that range from 80 to 103 cubic inches. You can choose the

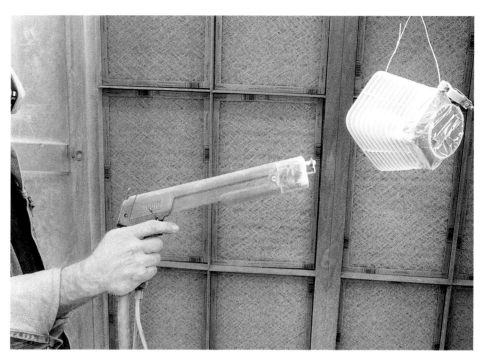

*Cylinders, heads and cases can be powder coated in almost any color imaginable to contrast or compliment the paint on the rest of the bike.*

*Think about the color of the engine as well as the color of the bike. Powder coating is extremely durable and adheres well to properly prepped aluminum.*

compression ratio, camshaft and even the style of timing gears, which will allow the use of modern electronic ignition.

The Panhead and early Shovelhead use what is essentially the same generator-style bottom end, so it's possible to add new Panheads from a company like STD, to the new Shovel cast iron cylinders. (see the Panhead chopper from Tank in Chapter Two as a good example of this method of Panhead building.) Before buying a genuine Panhead, remember that the newest of those old engines is over 35 years old. Be sure you understand what's involved in buying and maintaining an old engine.

About using Shovels in Evo frames, or the reverse, we offer the following comments from local expert, Jason Mitchell from Kokesh MC. Jason says the engine mounting pads are the same on a Shovelhead or an Evo-style V-twin: "The shovel will drop into the Evo frame," says Jason, "but to put an Evo in a Shovel frame you have to be sure the frame is tall enough. Evos are taller so height is the issue." For additional information on the use of a pre-Evo engine in your chopper see the interview with Tom Johnson from S&S.

We should mention that at least one additional firm makes complete new Shovelheads, Accurate Engineering. Berry Wardlaw from Accurate suggested we mention the fact that while most Evos won't fit into a stock Shovel frame, "we make one that does, it puts out 90 – 112 horsepower at the rear wheel and will bolt right in." For more on Accurate, see the comments farther along. Note: S&S also makes a very special Evo engine designed to fit Shovel frames.

## PUT THE SPORT BACK IN CHOPPERS

And as long as we're dealing here with new bikes designed to look old, we should mention the obvious: a lot of the old Choppers used a Sportster engine and transmission. You can still do that today as complete engines with integral transmission are available from your local Harley-Davidson dealer, though a frame that accepts the Sporty mill can be hard to find.

To quote George at Delano Harley-Davidson, "The 1200 engine in chrome is just over five thousand dollars, and it comes pretty complete, with the transmission and complete primary, the carb, ignition and charging circuit, but no air cleaner. The 883 engine is only $4457 retail and it comes with all the items I already mentioned."

Five thousand might seem like a lot of money, until you price a good Evo-style engine, plus the transmission, plus the primary, plus..... The only additional problem is the fact that most dealers don't stock the Sportster engines, so you will probably have to order one and wait for delivery.

Aftermarket Sportster cases are available from S&S, either in stock configuration for bore sizes up to 3-5/8 inch, or in special application form ready to accept cylinders with bores as large as 4 inches.

*From Cyril Huze comes this 100 cubic inch Pan based on 3-13/16 inch cylinders and 4-3/8 inch 'wheels. Includes a Super G carb and alternator.*

## THE REALLY OLD STUFF

Perhaps the best thing about motorcycles is the cast of characters that are drawn to this hobby/sport/obsession. Just because Harley Davidson hasn't made a Knucklehead for fifty years doesn't mean you can't buy one brand new, and better than the original, from the aftermarket. What follows are a few of the options available for anyone interested in running some classic American iron, Knuckleheads and Panheads, with a little information on some of the companies and individuals responsible for making these old designs available again.

## ACCURATE ENGINEERING

The Knucklehead is just one of the Signature Series V-Twins offered for sale by Berry Wardlaw, owner of Accurate Engineering. Berry explains that "we are strictly an engine building and testing facility."

Engine building includes everything from Knuckles to Evos and includes Panheads and Shovelheads. These are new engines, not rebuilt assemblies. The new Knuckleheads are assembled from special S&S cases with shafts from Jim's, ductile iron cylinders manufactured by Accurate (some smaller bore sizes use iron cylinders from an outside source) and heads from Knucklehead Power. Berry explains that the heads come in the door raw, "We do the finish machining on the ports, and install the guides and valves. The valves are manufactured for us by Black Diamond, they measure 1.940 inches for the intake and 1.750 for the exhaust. The guides we use allow us to use valve seals too, these are modern engines that can

*Said to combine "the look of the '50s without the oil leaks and blue smoke" these new Panheads come in 88, 93 and 103 inch sizes with generator or alternator. Accurate*

*This retro chopper from Tom Rad features the best of those old bikes, including a Sportster engine for power. New 883 and 1200 Sporty powerplants are available from any dealership.*

be used as daily transportation. The exhaust connection is the OEM slip-fit style, although we can weld on a three bolt flange if that's what the customer wants. Then we ship the engine with the exhaust pipe flange and the gasket."

By using a left side alternator-style case Accurate is able to ship engines with an alternator instead of a generator and there's an added benefit. "A 1970 and later inner primary will bolt right up," explains Berry, "so you can have late model primary drive and electric start."

If you fancy a new Knucklehead, Berry can put one together in various displacements ranging from 74 to 106 cubic inches. The 103 inch Knuckle, one of Berry's most popular models, uses a 4-1/2 inch stroke and 3-13/16 inch bore.

With a compression ratio of 9 to 1 these sleepers make 84 horses at the rear wheel.

Given the similarity between the Panhead and Knucklehead, it's not too surprising that Berry assembles and sells complete Panheads as well. In fact one of their 103 inch Panheads in a mild state of tune was documented to put out 91 horsepower and 94 foot pounds of torque at only 4100 RPM, enough to surprise many an Evo or Twin-Cam rider. Though some of the components come from different sources, the basic program and the possible displacements are similar to those offered for the Knucklehead.

## PANZER MOTORCYCLE WORKS

In some ways similar to Knucklehead Power, Panzer is a motorcycle manufacturing company built around one particular style of V-twin engine. In this case that style is the Panhead. Their Neo-Pan engine is based on a set of S&S cases filled with S&S 'wheels and shafts and a specially machined billet gearcase cover. From the cases up these engines are mostly S&S components topped with a set of flowed STD heads. The heads come with the three-bolt flange, not the OEM-style slip-on exhaust connection.

The typical Panzer engine displaces 90 cubic inches, achieved by using 4-3/8 inch 'wheels and 3-5/8 inch cylinders. Like many new/old engines, the Panzer mill uses an alternator, though real generators, supplied by Cycle Electric, are available by special request.

*What some call the best looking engine to come out of Milwaukee, these new Knuckleheads are available in gloss black finish with polished highlights. Sizes up to 106 cubic inches to surprise your neighbor on his TC 88. Accurate*

## KNUCKLEHEAD POWER

Tony Pierce, owner of Knucklehead Power USA, describes himself as a Knucklehead fanatic and his company doesn't make anything but Knuckleheads. Tony's long-time dream was to re-introduce the Knucklehead and he's done exactly that. Unlike some of the other firms in this section, Knucklehead Power manufactures complete motorcycles, powered by their own Knucklehead engine. The bikes they sell include everything from a Time Warp Chopper to a Deluxe model with electric start and foot shift.

By forming a partnership with Flathead Power, a Swedish firm, Tony is able to import the heads and many other components manufactured in Sweden. What they call their "production" engine displaces 84 cubic inches and

*To make these easier to run in modern chassis the sprocket shafts are longer than a stock Pan. Ignition is modern Uni-Lite from Mallory. Left side case is designed to accept an alternator. CSI*

Tony swears it will smoke an Evo. Almost any size, shape and configuration of V-Twin can be ordered, as long as it's a Knucklehead. Street versions of their Knucklehead come with alternator left cases and a generator right case, so a modern 32 amp alternator can be used.

Knucklehead Power might be sub-titled KnucklesXtreme. "We take Knuckles to the limit," is how Tony describes some of their work. If an 84 or 103 cubic inch engine isn't quite fast enough, how about a 130 cubic inch Knucklehead, or a Knuckle with a blower, or a Knuckle with a carburetor hanging off either side? If you can dream it up, Tony and crew can probably build it.

*Pan-demonium is the name, making Panheads available once again is the game. Built specifically for Chrome Specialties, these new/old engines displace 88 cubic inches. CSI*

## PAN-DEMONIUM

In closing this section on Engines we need to mention the other major source of new Panheads: Chrome Specialties. "Pan-demonium" is a complete 88 cubic inch Pan-style V-twin utilizing 3-5/8 inch cast iron cylinders and 4-1/4 inch flywheel assembly, both sourced from RevTech. Dual-plug cylinder heads come from STD, the E series carb from S&S, the .470 inch camshaft from Andrews and the hydraulic lifters from Jim's. By using a late-style left side case and sprocket shaft, "Pan-demonium" engines are compatible with 1970 and up inner primaries and either four or five-speed transmissions. In lieu of a generator, these Pan-style engines use a modern stator and rotor located in the left side case. More information on these engines can be found by contacting your local CSI dealer.

## Q&A WITH TOM JOHNSON FROM S&S

With over thirty years of experience riding and wrenching on Harleys, and fifteen years writing for *American Iron Magazine*, Tom Johnson from S&S is in a unique position to explain some of the options available for anyone wishing to run a pre-Evo engine in their new Chopper. As Tom explains, you don't have to go scrounging through the swap meet if you want a Shovelhead or Panhead, as new examples of either motor are as close as your S&S catalog.

*Tom, tell us a little bit about the Shovelheads that S&S sells, what kind of options does the buyer have?*

We do alternator and generator-style cases, we can even build them with an alternator left side and generator right case so you get the looks of an older engine. You even get the whine of the old engines, which sounds pretty cool.

Displacements range from 80 to 103 cubic inches, but the 93 is probably the best combination. That has a 4-1/2 inch stroke and a 3-5/8 inch bore with either cast or forged pistons. I replaced an old 74 with a 93 in one of my old bikes and the 93 inch engine was smoother and had way more power, it's a better motor all the way around.

*Will either style of case drop into a typical aftermarket frame designed for an Evo.*

Yes, the bottom mounts are the same, the only glitch can be the top motor mount. Ours is two-piece mount. In a worst case scenario you might have to do some minor fabrication there. The generator case isn't an issue in terms of fitment, but pipes can be an issue, especially with our custom engines that use an Evo-style top end on a generator bottom. There you'll need a custom made outside-the-frame pipe because the generator bulge is right there where a typical

*Built by Berry Wardlaw for a personal project, this Evo in a factory four-speed frame proves that old dogs can learn new tricks - and that not all Evos are too tall for Shovelhead frames. Accurate*

*New complete Shovelheads are available from S&S. Options include high performance titanium top collars and dual plugs.*

five-speed box. If you had a four-speed frame, you would want to go with one of the "five-speed in a four-seed box" transmissions that are available from different sources. The thing to bear in mind there is that your clutch has to be compatible with the tranny mainshaft and main drive gear. Rear belt drives complicate things too.

It's tempting to pick up any good deals that you stumble across at a late-Shovel or Evo front pipe makes the bend through the frame.

*If I buy generator style, are the generators and regulators readily available?*

You bet. To me, the only source for generators is Cycle Electric in Ohio. Most of the major distributors carry Cycle Electric parts. If you don't see the name, the CE generator will be listed as American-made. Cycle Electric also makes solid state regulators which are way more reliable than the old Harley regulators.

*What about the primary housing and primary drive for one of these Shovelheads. How does a person get the right combination of primary parts.*

Shaft lengths are the main thing to watch for when mixing and matching driveline components. The basic year groups are 1936 – 1964, 1965 to 1969, and '70 up for the Shovel and Evo engine sprocket shafts. The sprocket shaft and transmission mainshaft have to be compatible lengths.

The 1970 – up Shovel and Evo engines would work with a Harley 5-speed if you had the right clutch and the frame was set up for the

*Complete Evo style engines based on 3-1/2 and 3-5/8 inch bores can be matched with stroker flywheels to produce displacements up to 103 cubic inches (3-5/8X 5). S&S*

swap meet or whatever and just hope for the best. But, you'll probably run into fewer headaches if you pick a year group for the primary drive and starter and just stick with it when you're buying parts.

Some of the five speed kicker kits are a little iffy for day-in, day-out riding, and I'd probably use a four-speed transmission if I were going to build a kick-only bike. I've heard that the five-speed kicker kits from Billet Bilt and Sharp Eye Engineering are good, but I've never used one myself.

*Complete alternator style Shovelhead engines can be purchased with compression ratios up to 9.5 to 1, and displacements of 80 to 103 cubic inches. S&S*

With primary covers, you have to match the inner primary to your left engine case and the transmission case. The starter assembly and starter drive have to be compatible with the inner primary cover or starter mount, and the ring gear on the clutch shell.

I've had the best luck with Spyke and OEM Harley starters. One thing you do not want to do is buy an import copy of the old Prestolite or OEM Hitachi starters. They just don't have the power or durability that the originals did. Also, remember that electric start batteries are much bigger than kick only batteries, and you'll need a place to put your battery. Electric start batteries won't fit in the stock horseshoe oil tanks or exact copies.

*Can the S&S generator Shovelhead be combined with aftermarket heads to create a new "Panhead?"*

Yes. What I would do is start with the S&S generator-shovel Long Block, minus heads. Then I would order Pan-style heads from STD, which fit the Shovel cylinders as well as the Pan. The rockers are available from either Ted's or Panzer. The STD heads are pretty good and they will accept the stock pans. They do use a three bolt exhaust flange that some people don't like. The original engines had a slip-on exhaust spigot but those would sometimes crack if the pipe wasn't clamped in place correctly.

*Is there a downside to using a Shovelhead, especially a generator-Shovelhead, in place of an Evo?*

There are more parts so generator-Shovels are a little more expensive to build. The generator Shovel might be 300 to 500 dollars more expensive. For people who want a classic motor that will run coast to coast, a Shovel is the one. The main advantage of an Evo is, it's more oil tight. And the aluminum cylinders dissipate heat better. Shovel rings and pistons run hotter and don't last as long. Modern Shovels go 35,000 to 50,000 miles before needing a top-end job. Most Evos go way past that.

And you may not want to run a generator because alternators do tend to last longer and be more trouble free. As I said, S&S can combine a generator right case with an alternator left case. That way you can use the more modern alternator. Some old-school guys keep the generator in there just in case. Others block it off and mount the oil filter there.

What's really neat is the Evo that we build on a set of Generator cases, that's a unique engine, and good looking too.

*An unusual combination of parts allows you to run an alternator or generator in the early style bottom end with a modern Evo-style top end. S&S*

69

## Chapter Six

# Drivetrain Options

## Belts & Chains & Transmissions

Choppers are choppers. Which means that no two bikes are alike. If everyone ran an Evo engine with five-speed transmission, we wouldn't even need this chapter. The fact is there are at least five different engine types being used today, and three trans-

missions. And then there's right side drive to consider. Whether you want to run a four speed in a five-speed case, or belt primary, we've tried to outline the most popular possibilities, along with the advantages and possible pitfalls. In many cases it isn't that you

*Rather than hassle with choices over engine, transmission and primary drive, RevTech makes complete kits available that incude everything you need for a soft-tail type drivetrain. No more worries about which inner primary or starter, it's all here: 88 or 100 inch engine, 5 or 6-speed tranny, complete primary with Kevlar clutch. CCI*

can't combine a particular engine with a particular transmission in a particular frame, it's just easier if you don't. As always, it's best to think first and buy parts second.

## TRANSMISSION CONSIDERATIONS

Most builders are going to use a five or six-speed transmission. When using earlier style engines however you may want to use the earlier four-speed transmission. To quote Jason from Kokesh MC, "The frame will determine the transmission. Some rigid frames will take a four or five-speed transmission. In that case the five-speed would be a soft-tail style five-speed." Before running out to buy a complete four-speed transmission consider the fact that a complete four-speed may not be less expensive than a complete five-speed.

There are transmission mounting plates from Paughco (and possibly other sources as well) that allow you to put a soft-tail-style five-speed in a four-speed frame. This option doesn't always work well with wide tires and transmission offsets, however. Some frames, like those from Santee, will accept four, five or six-speed transmissions, you simply have to use the correct transmission mounting plate.

You can put a five-speed in a four-speed frame with a special transmission case from S&S or Custom Chrome or one of the other large warehouses. You can also buy these transmissions complete from a number of sources. The downside is the fact that they all use an early five-speed gearset. This means you have to use the earlier clutch assembly instead of the typical late-style clutch and hub assembly. The earlier clutch assemblies aren't nearly as strong as the later model clutches used by the factory.

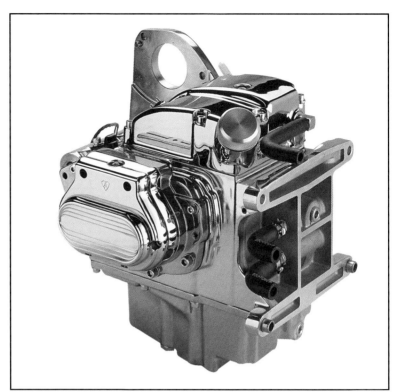

*Transmissions meant for use behind a TC 88 have a very different shape that earlier models. These complete assemblies are available with polished cases, with or without extended mainshaft for 250 tire applications. Ness*

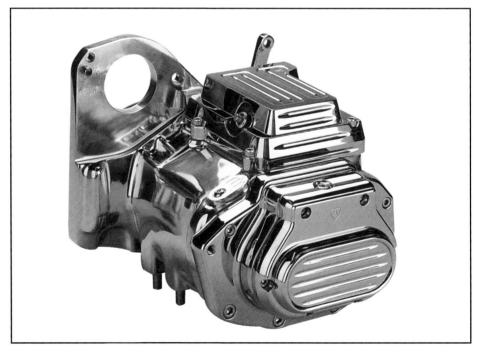

*Soft-tail style 5 and 6-speed transmissions are available with Baker or Zodiac gears, polished and with chrome top cover and side covers. Ness*

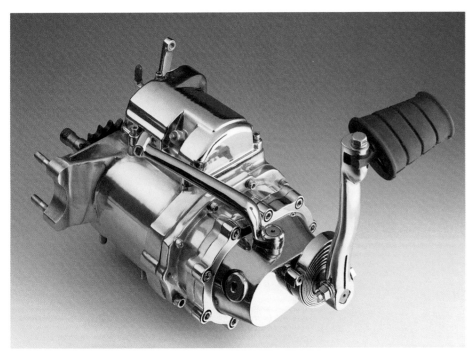

*This four speed transmission case houses an early-style five speed gear set. Fits four speed frames and 1970 and up inner primaries. Designed for chain final drive. CCI*

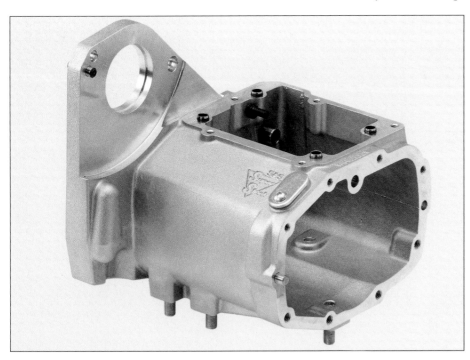

*Cast from 356 aluminum, this soft-tail style transmission case will accept various 5 or 6-speed gearsets. Includes the port (on the right side) for the electronic speedo sensor. S&S*

These won't stand up to the big inch engines many of us now take for granted. Rivera does offer the very durable Pro-clutch for both four-speed and early five-speed transmissions.

And as long as we are delving into this gray area of using "old shit" to build a new motorcycle, there are the additional issues of kick start. Kick start kits for five-speed transmissions are available from CCI and perhaps other sources as well. "The trouble with kickers," explains Jason, "is the exhaust. Unless you use early Softail exhaust (from the days when factory Softails came with a kicker) the kicker runs into most current exhaust systems. It might be easier to have custom pipes manufactured. The other problem is the ignition, most current ignition systems are designed for electric start." Many of the five-speed in a four-speed case transmissions can be ordered with a kicker.

## FIVE-SPEED TRANSMISSIONS

Most aftermarket frames designed for pre-TC engines will accept a typical late-model five-speed transmission. These are available in any catalog that's on the counter at the local parts store.

You can also buy complete transmissions from any Harley-Davidson dealer. Harley-Davidson made a major change in their transmissions in about 1994 when they began the conversion to high contact gears. Ground in such a way as to reduce noise and increase strength, these gears can't be mixed with other non HCR gears.

Softail-style five-speed cases are nearly the same from 1986 to 1999. Factory transmissions built prior to 1990 used a tapered mainshaft, which required the appropriate clutch basket. Thus the most common complete five-speed transmissions are often listed as 1990 – 1999.

## SIX-SPEEDS

Baker Transmission was the first to introduce a six-speed transmission in 1998. Today there are at least two other firms making six-speed transmissions. The beauty of these transmissions with the extra gear is the fact that the case is the same as a five-speed case, and the mainshaft is the same as a five-speed mainshaft. So a primary assembly that works with a late-model five-speed will work just as well with a new six-speed. For the same reason, six-speed gearsets will fit into a standard five-speed case.

The Baker transmission is available with either a .86 or .80 to 1 overdrive ratio, which will drop the RPM at 70 mph by 475 and 680 RPM respectively. The RevTech six-speed transmission comes with a sixth gear ratio of .893 to one.

## SPEEDOMETERS.

All late model bikes from the factory use electronic speedometers, "driven" by a pickup in the transmission. Obviously you have to decide during the early part of the planning process whether your speedometer will be electronic or mechanical. Assuming, that is, you've decided to use a speedo at all. Nearly all new complete five and six-speed transmissions have the correct gears and the small port to accept the sensor. The factory began the switch to electronic speedometers in 1994, so earlier transmissions, or transmissions listed in the catalog as "1991 to 1994 Softail" might not be equipped to drive an electronic speedometer.

Bert Baker from Baker transmissions reports that all their five and six-speed transmissions, "have the right gearset to trigger the sensor, and the cases are machined to physically accept the sensor." Earlier five-speed cases, equipped with the right gearset (actually it's fourth gear), can be machined to accept the sensor. Lee Wickstrom at Lee's Speed Shop has a fixture for this, but it's a fair amount of work.

Electronic speedometers have a number of advantages. There is no ugly cable running from the front wheel to the handle bars or up between the tanks. And calibration is never a problem, no matter which front tire you use with which speedo drive assembly. Many of the newest speedometers will accept the signal from a factory sensor as well as their own, and self calibrate without the need for a separate calibration box. Some transmission/sensor /speedometer combinations will require a recalibration box between the sensor and the speedometer head.

For anyone who wants to run a mechanical speedometer there are two basic styles and three ratios. One-to-one speedometers were used with transmission-driven speedometers in four-speed

*You can convert that 5-speed transmission to a 6-speed with this Baker by Jim's 6-speed gearset. Ness*

*The Pro Clutch is a great upgrade for anyone running a 4 or early 5-speed drivetrain. Rivera*

*Some electronic speedometer installations require a brain box like this to calibrate the speedometer. S&S*

bikes and can probably be eliminated from consideration for anyone building a new bike. Two-to-one speedometers were used mostly with FX and FXR bikes equipped with nineteen inch front wheels and narrow glide forks. A third ratio, 2240:1, was used with Softails with twenty one inch front wheels and wide glide forks.

The trick is to match the front end, the forks and the wheel diameter, to the right style of drive unit. Then match that drive unit to a speedometer with a matching ratio. Now all you need is the right cable in the right length with the correct fittings on either end. Confusion can be minimized by spending a little time with one of the big catalogs, or a good counter person at your local shop.

## PRIMARY COLORS

Primary assemblies definitely come in more than three colors. In fact, connecting the engine with the transmission, and choosing the matching inner and outer housing, along with matching starter and hardware, can be downright confusing.

As Jason from Kokesh likes to say: "The engine and transmission will determine the primary." If this is a case of a standard issue Evo and five-speed, then you have the option of running the standard chain-style primary with all the matching components.

But even for a simple application like a late-model Evo and five-speed you still have to get the right inner and outer primary covers, with the finish you need, designed for forward controls, along with the compensator sprocket, the chain itself, matching clutch assembly and matching starter motor. Because all of these components have to work together, a number of companies now offer "kits" that include matching components for late-model applications.

Among these kits is a complete primary assembly, without a starter, from Biker's Choice for 1989 to 1993 Softails and another for 1994 – 2000 Softails. Custom Chrome offers very similar kits, with or without heavy duty Kevlar clutch. All factory bikes from 1994 on use the same gear-reduction starter, so by using the 1994 and later inner and outer primary you could also use the latest starter.

And therein lies the rub. In addition to buying an inner primary that will match up to the bolt pattern on both the engine and transmission, you also have to determine which is the right starter and which set of sprocket/chain/clutch-hub will work. As

Tom Johnson mentions in his interview in Chapter Four, life is easier is you stay within certain year groupings. There are still differences within the year groupings, and cases where there are two or more outer primaries used with a certain inner primary.

For older pre-Evo engines, there are no complete kits. You have to match the transmission to the frame, and then find the right inner primary to connect the two. The clutch hub must match the transmission mainshaft. Though new Shovelheads can likely be matched up with five-speed transmissions through the use of a 1970 and up inner primary, it's a good idea to buy all the parts from one shop. There are some subtle differences in the engine/inner primary connection on some engines. And not all inner primaries are compatible with belt final drive. If the engine is a Shovel, mated to a five-speed with belt final drive, a 1989 to 1993 Softail inner and outer primary would work, with the matching one-piece starter.

## OPEN PRIMARY

Seldom do choppers use standard issue components. Near the top of the must-have list for many chopper builders is the open primary. Open as in, little or no housing to contain the belt. As in, keep your pants legs away from all the spinning machinery.

Belts come in a variety of widths, some narrow enough to fit inside a conventional inner and outer primary housing, some so wide there aren't

*If you want to run a speedometer but don't want a huge gauge hanging on the handle bars, consider the mini speedo. Only 1-7/8 inch in diameter can be combined with matching tach and installed in a variety of housings. Ness*

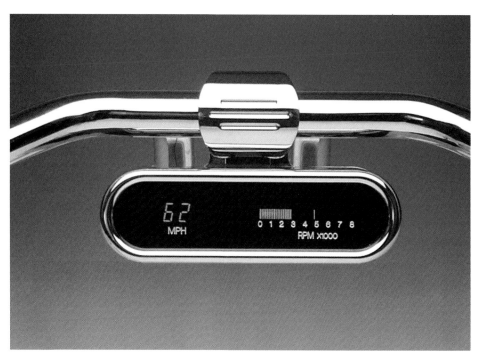

*Join the digital age. This Dakota Digital gauge combines a speedometer and bar-graph tachometer. Use it with mechanical or electronic input. Ness*

75

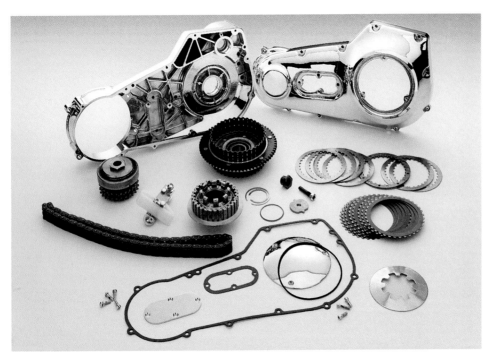

any housings big enough to house them. Both BDL, Primo and Karata offer primary drive assemblies that include engine sprocket, belt and clutch assembly, designed to replace a conventional chain primary. For more on belt primaries, check out the interview with John Ventriglia from Primo Belt Drives.

*Kits like these make it easier to get the right parts without 6 trips to the parts store. Includes the complete late model inner and outer primary for soft-tail chassis and can be ordered with heavy duty clutch. CCI*

## OFFSET DRIVETRAINS AND RSD
### Offset Drivetrains

Installing a fat tire in an existing bike or frame, or designing a frame to accept a 200 series or bigger tire, often involves offsetting the transmission, or transmission and engine, to the left. The basic problem is the fact that as rear tires get wider they inevitably run into the belt.

To create some clearance between the new tire and the belt the frame manufacturer must move the tire/wheel to the right or the belt to the left. Most frames that accept 200 and wider rear tires make room for the belt by offsetting the transmission, and sometimes the engine, to the left.

Offsetting the transmission requires a short discussion of the drivetrain on a typical hardtail or soft-tail style frame. While the new TC 88B motors use an essentially unitized engine and transmission, the earlier non-rubber-mount Evo engines connect to the transmission only on the left side through the inner and outer primary and the primary drive itself. What this means is that it's relatively easy to offset

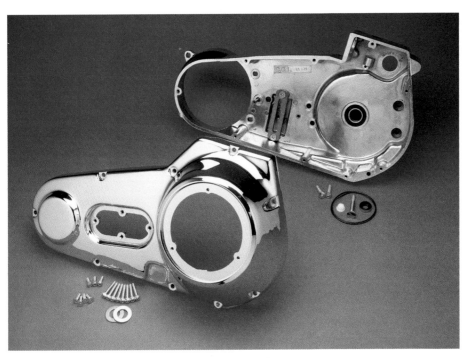

*These chrome inner and outer primary covers are designed for 1970 to 1988 4-speed drivetrains and are reinforced at all major stress points. Can be used with chain or belt final drive. CCI*

the transmission to the left while leaving the engine in the center, or close to center, of the frame.

The first Wide Tire Kits consisted of a spacer used between the left side of the engine and the inside of the inner primary, an offset transmission mounting plate, and a spacer for the compensating sprocket. Those early kits moved the transmission over 1/4 or 1/2 inch, while the new range of kits move the transmission as much as an inch. As the belt steps farther and farther to the left though it eventually hits the frame.

In the case of complete frames or frame and swingarm kits, most of the new offerings from the aftermarket are specifically designed to accept the wide tires we all take for granted. Most have a wider rear section so there's room for the wide tire, with transmission (possibly engine mounts as well) mounts offset to the left enough so there's room between the wheel and the tire for a full 1-1/2 inch belt. Many of these frames include the offset kit as part of the frame package you buy.

You can only move all that weight so far to the left though before you affect the balance of the bike. This is not static weight either, but spinning weight with it's own gyroscopic effect. The way to avoid this potential imbalance is to limit the size of the rear tire, use chain drive or consider a RSD frame and drivetrain.

## Right side drive

As discussed above, wider and wider tires typically mean transmission and drivetrain offsets farther and farther to the

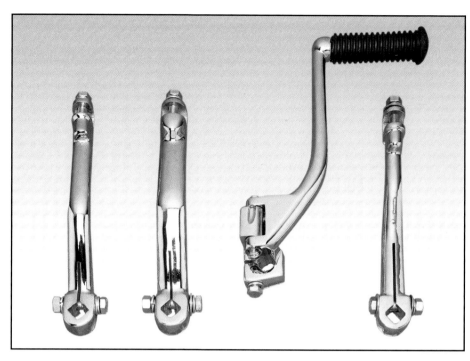

*Kicker shafts and pedals often get in the way of the exhaust (maybe it's the other way around). These kick arm assemblies are designed to make it easier to run store-bought exhaust on a kick start bike. CCI*

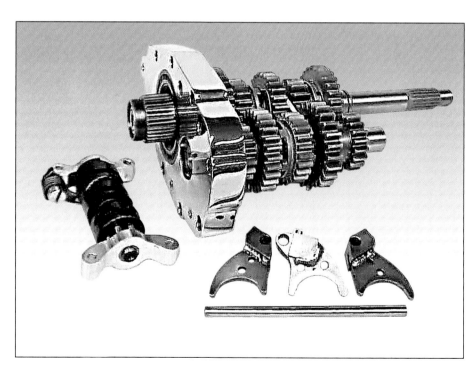

*This RSD gearset fits standard 5-speed cases and moves the final drive to the right side. Available in 5 and 6-speed configurations. Baker*

left. The solution to ever-expanding offsets is a right hand drive transmission. Baker, first to market with a six-speed transmission a few years ago, is offering for sale both five and six-speed transmissions with right hand drive. By moving the final drive to the bike's right side (these are big twins, not Sportsters) you minimize the need to use spacers to move the primary drive and transmission to the left. The result is a more balanced motorcycle.

"Now you don't have the transmission set way over on the left side," explains Bert Baker. "And the engine drive sprocket isn't spinning way out there an inch or more away from the case. When we did the first prototypes I thought this would be a fringe-deal, only a few of the top builders would be interested. But the response has been surprising. We had eight frame manufacturers making compatible frames, including American Thunder, Daytec, and West Coast Chopper, but there are more than that now."

*Right side drive transmissions must be installed in RSD frames, and then combined with the correct pulley, wheel and rear brake. Shown here is a RSD soft-tail style bike being assembled at American Thunder based on a Rolling Thunder frame.*

This new transmission uses many standard five-speed parts, and a standard five-speed case, though the shift drum and forks, main and counter shafts and fifth (and sixth) gear are specific to the new right-side transmission. Like their standard five and six-speed transmission, the gears inside this new RSD transmission are manufactured by Andrews. The chassis used must be set up to run right-side drive.

*Whether it's RSD or not, soft-tail style drive trains make it easy to offset the transmission because the engine and transmission are connected together only through the primary housing.*

## FINAL DRIVE OPTIONS
### Belts and Chains.

When it comes to transferring power from one shaft to another, the toothed belt offers the efficiency of a chain without the mess or maintenance. Up until the introduction of the 2000 models the Big Twins used a 1-1/2 inch belt while the Sportster line used a 1-1/8 inch belt. The larger belt worked well for all but the most twisted rider and stood up to all but the worst abuse without stripping or breaking.

The use of big-bore aftermarket engines of 113 and 121 cubic inches with 130 or more horsepower has changed the durability of belt drive. A rider who likes to twist the wrist can now break a standard 1-1/2 inch belt. This doesn't mean you can't mix belt drive with big engines. Some riders with big engines have no trouble at all. It depends on how you ride and probably the weight of the bike. Troubles with belts has turned the spotlight on an earlier form of power transmission.

### The Chain-drive Gang

An increasing number of bikes are showing up with chains in place of the belt. Despite their need for additional maintenance, chains retain some definite advantages, especially when it comes to choppers: They leave more room for fat tires and make it easy to change final drive ratios. Certain transmissions, like a four-speed or five in a four-speed box, also lend themselves to chain final drive.

Because these are choppers and less likely to be ridden cross country, the maintenance issue might not be such a big deal. Most of the better chains come with O-rings to lock in the factory lube. Some riders just use silicone spray, in lieu of conventional chain-lube, which keeps the O-rings soft. You can even buy a chain with nickel plated side plates for a nice look. The nice thing about using a chain final drive on a chopper is the raw or retro dimension they add to the bike. A number of firms and catalogs offer offset transmission sprockets to help move the chain far enough to the left to clear the rear tire.

Whether or not you use chain drive will be part of the overall plan for the bike. Ask yourself, how hard do I ride, are the components old or old-style, am I searching for that real stripped-to-the-bone aura the real old choppers had? Then make a decision about the final drive.

## INTERVIEW: JOHN, VENTRIGLIA FROM PRIMO BELT DRIVES.

*John, can you tell us a little about Primo and Rivera and your involvement with Primo.*

Primo and Rivera are separate corporations but occupy the same building. I own part of Primo Belt Drives, I've been involved since 1973. I do assembly, installation and prototyping of all the new kits. And I'm vice president of both corporations.

*John, let's start by talking about enclosed belt drives. How do these compare to OEM type chain primary drives and what are some of the advantages?*

Well, if the guy has a Softail with a five or six-speed our belt kits cost about the same amount as a chain primary. The belt actually acts as a shock absorber, for smoother power transmission, and the clutch is much better than the OEM clutch. The belt is lighter, so you loose some unwanted pounds. When we sell a kit, everything needed is included. We can set them up to work with either a 1990 to

*A 200X16 on the right has nearly the same overall diameter as the 250X18 on the left. CCI*

This 3 inch open belt drive is designed for electric start and comes with the two-part motor plate (inner primary) and all necessary pulleys and the clutch assembly. Rivera

1993 starter, or a 1994 and later starter.

*What about open belt drives. What are the advantages?*

Mainly it's the appearance. The belts are wide and as a result stronger. When you have 120 cubic inches or more, it's a good idea to go to either a 3 inch or 3-1/2 inch 14mm belt. The pack contains up to eight clutch plates, and of course there is no oil in the primary to leak. When running an open belt drive it is important to use a belt guard as recommended by Primo.

*Can you talk about your motor plate and how you fit the right plate to the right engine and tranny combination?*

The motor plate configuration is dependent upon which motor and transmission is being used, with the transmission being the main factor. Our original motorplate was designed as a two-piece unit allowing easier fitment with custom or non OEM machines. With a one-piece plate it is almost always required that the motor or transmission be shimmed to fit correctly. Our two-piece motor plate is as strong or stronger than most one-piece plates. You can actually pick up the motorcycle by using the motorplate. We offer four different two-piece motorplates to fit Shovelheads, FXR, Dyna and Softail motor-

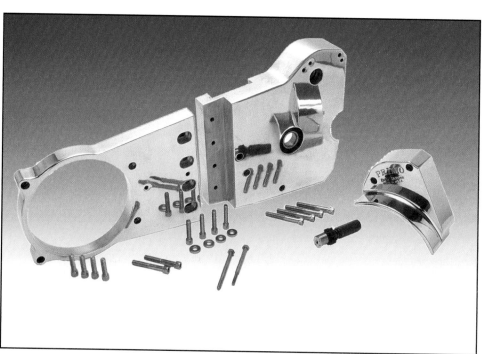

Two part motor plates are available to fit most engine/transmission combinations. Design means that even if the engine/transmission alignment is off slightly you won't have to shim the transmission. Rivera

cycles. We also offer a new one-piece motor plate for use with our new 3-1/2 inch wide Brute V Twin Cam belt drive kit.

*How does the belt drive gear ratio compare to the stock chain-type primary, and what are the belts themselves made from?*

Our gear ratios are very close to stock, the Brute III for example (enclosed 1-3/4 inch wide belt drive system) has a drive ratio of 1.5 to 1. We use Aramid fibers belts because they withstand the heavy shock loads better. Belt breakage is rare.

*What are the mistakes people make when they buy or install a belt drive?*

They go to the swap meet and get what they think is a good deal. Then the parts don't fit correctly. If you don't know what you're doing or what you're buying, you should not buy it. Swap meet buyers sometimes call me complaining they have pulley combinations that we don't ship or manufacture and want to exchange or replace them. It's not as simple as it may seem to the ordinary rider. It's best to purchase a belt drive kit from a reputable or well known dealer or manufacturer. Deal with a company that's been around awhile. You might pay a little more, but fitment and quality are guaranteed. We back what we sell, no exceptions.

*The Brute II is designed to replace the primary chain on pre-Evo/4-speed applications. Comes with 11mm belt and a Pro Clutch. Rivera*

*A variety of belt guards and clutch hub covers are available to dress up your open belt installation. Rivera*

## Chapter Seven

# Get Wired

## Not Murphy's Law, Ohm's Law

To better understand some basics of motor-cycle electrical systems and why they are designed the way they are, there are a few basic terms we need to understand and an explanation of each one.

FIRST, THE TERMS.
Voltage (V): the force that pushes electrons through a wire (sometimes called the electromotive force).
Current (I): the volume of electrons moving

*At Donnie Smith Custom Cycles they like to use a coil bracket with ignition and dimmer switch which makes for a simple and compact harness. And wherever possible they run the wires inside the frame tubes. The effect is very neat and still very functional. Harnesses are made up using factory wiring colors.*

through the wire, measured in amps.

Resistance (R): the restriction to the flow of electrons measured in ohms.

Most people have heard of the "water through the hose theory." In this analogy the water pressure is the voltage, the volume of water is the current and the kink in the hose is the resistance.

The way these three forces interact is contained in a very simple formula you may remember from Science or Physics class, known as Ohm's law.

Ohm's law: V=IxR or stated another way, I =V/R and R=V/I

## THE IMPORTANCE OF WIRE SIZE

The size of wire is very important to the flow of electrons. The larger the wire, with more strands in the wire, the more current it can carry. Different wire sizes and types are manufactured with different amounts of strands. Most household wire is made of a single heavy strand, good for carrying high voltages and low current. In automotive and motorcycle applications the wire is sized from light to heavy and is always made up of many strands, which is good for carrying higher current flows at relatively low voltage. Multiple strands also makes the wire flexible and less prone to breakage from vibration.

The size of a wire is known as its gauge. It's one of those inverse relationships: bigger

## Recommended Wire Sizes

| Length<br>Current | 0-4 ft. | 4-7 ft. | 7-10 ft. | 10-13 ft. | 13-16 ft. | 16-19 ft. |
|---|---|---|---|---|---|---|
| 0-20A | 14 ga. | 12 ga. | 12 ga. | 10 ga. | 10 ga. | 8 ga. |
| 20-35A | 12 ga. | 10 ga. | 8 ga. | 8 ga. | 6 ga. | 6 ga. |
| 35-50A | 10 ga. | 8 ga. | 8 ga. | 6 ga. | 6 ga. | 4 ga. |
| 50-65A | 8 ga. | 8 ga. | 6 ga. | 4 ga. | 4 ga. | 4 ga. |
| 65-85A | 6 ga. | 6 ga. | 4 ga. | 4 ga. | 2 ga. | 2 ga. |
| 85-105A | 6 ga. | 6 ga. | 4 ga. | 2 ga. | 2 ga. | 2 ga. |
| 105-125A | 4 ga. | 4 ga. | 4 ga. | 2 ga. | 2 ga. | 0 ga. |
| 125-150A | 2 ga. | 2 ga. | 2 ga. | 2 ga. | 0 ga. | 0 ga. |

*How heavy a wire you need for particular circuit depends on both the amount of current and the length of the wire.*

*Both 32 and 22 amp regulators are available in the billet model as shown. Ness*

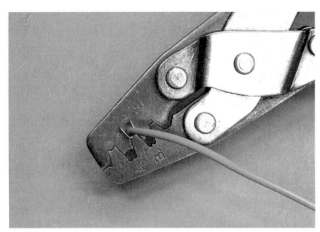

*A good crimp on the small pins used in factory type terminal blocks is a two step process. First you have to crimp the pin onto the stripped wire.*

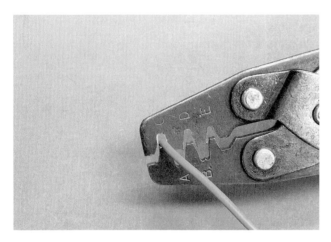

*Part two, done in a different set of "jaws," crimps the outer part of the pin onto the wire's insulation.*

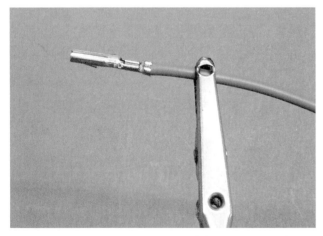

*Note the neat two part crimp. If done correctly the joint is strong and will slide easily into the terminal block.*

numbers indicate a smaller wire able to carry less current. A 22 gauge wire might be used for a gauge or small bulb while a 4 or 6 gauge wire would make a good motorcycle battery cable.

Higher quality wire generally contains a larger number of smaller diameter strands. As a general rule of thumb always use the highest number of strands per wire size as possible.

### How Big Should the Wire be?

The two things that determine the gauge of wire needed in a particular circuit are the current load the wire will need to carry, and the length of the wire that carries that load (see the wire size chart). More current requires a larger diameter wire (smaller gauge number). The same current, but in a longer piece of wire, will require a larger diameter wire. When in doubt about the diameter of the wire you need for particular application always go larger, not smaller.

The other thing to consider when buying wire is the quality of the insulation. The best automotive grade wire is TXL, with insulation that is thinner, yet more heat (125 degrees C) and abrasion resistant than anything else on the market. A more common rating might be GPT, this is common "auto store" wire with insulation rated at 85 degrees C.

Remember that the new high temperature insulation like that used with TXL is thinner than the insulation used with lesser grades of wire making it hard to determine the gauge of the wire. What looks at first like a 16 gauge wire might actually be 14 gauge wire with the new, thinner insulation.

## PROTECT WIRING AND COMPONENTS
### Fuses

A fuse is one of the most important parts of the electrical circuit. The fuse is the weak link in the passage of current and is designed to allow only a preset amount of current to flow through the circuit. By using a fuse, damage to sensitive electronic parts and powered circuits can be avoided. A fuse is simply a small conductive strip between two contacts, designed to melt at a certain temperature. When current flow reaches a certain maximum level, the natural resistance of the strip creates enough heat to melt the strip, which stops the current flow. If a hot wire rubs through the insulation and contacts the frame, the fuse will blow well before the wire gets hot enough to melt. Without a fuse (or circuit breaker) you run the risk of melting the wires in one or more circuits and possibly starting a fire.

### Circuit Breakers

Circuit breakers, like fuses, are designed to protect circuits from overloading. The major difference is that fuses are not reusable and circuit breakers are. Circuit breakers have a bimetallic strip that heats up under overload conditions. Because the small strip is made up of two different metals, they expand at different rates when hot, which causes the strip to warp, pulling the contacts apart and breaking the circuit.

Most of the circuit breakers used with V-twins are what you might call automatic reset. This type of circuit breaker will automatically reset itself when the bimetallic strip cools. This is the most commonly used type and will continue to turn current off and on as long as the circuit is overloaded.

Physically smaller circuit breakers are available in the standard 15 and 30 amp ratings. The smaller size makes it easier to neatly locate these breakers when wiring custom bikes.

### RELAYS AND SOLENOIDS
#### Relays

A relay can be thought of as a remote switch controlled by another switch. Most relays have two "sides," a control side and a load side (check the illustration). In most cases, when you hit the switch you put current through the control

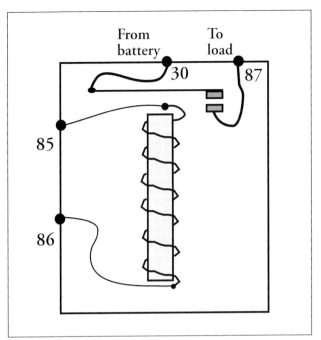

A relay is really just a remote switch. When a relatively small current moves through the control side (terminals 85 and 86) a magnitic field is created which pulls down the armature and closes the load side of the relay (terminals 30 and 87). Solid-state relays eliminate the moving parts and points but work just the same.

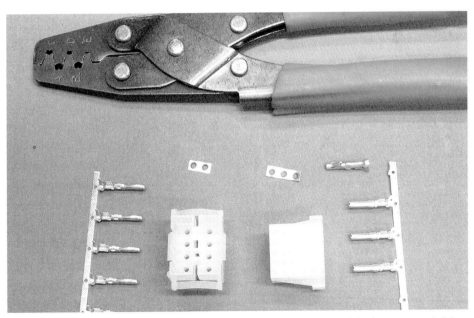

The crimper shown is known as "GM style." The terminal blocks are available from dealerships or the aftermarket. Factory type harnesses use terminal blocks to connect handlebar harnesses to the main harness. Don Tima uses them behind the coil bracket on customs - so the coil and ignition switch can be easily pulled off for service.

# Soldering 101

These are Don Tima's tools of the trade: rosin core solder, flux for cleaning and a bracket to act as an extra hand.

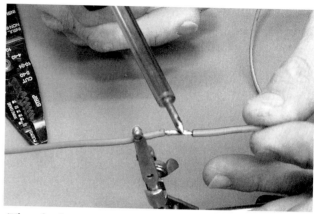

Then he brings together the two tinned ends and applies heat and more solder as needed. This is just as strong as a twisted splice.

He strips the insulation first, with the correct tool not a pocket knife. Then he dips the bare end in the flux.

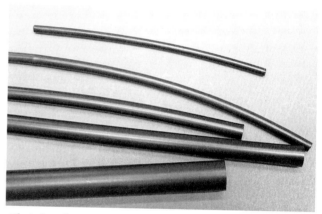

Shrink tube comes in various sizes including waterproof examples.

Don likes to "tin" each end: heat the bare wire and solder so liquid solder is absorbed by and coats all the strands.

Following application of heat the tubing shrinks around the splice. Note that Don's splice is only marginally larger than the surrounding wire.

side of the relay which then closes the contacts on the load side.

A relay is designed to pass relatively large amounts of current to specific devices, rather than have that current pass through switches and major harnesses. Relays are often used to prevent overloading of circuits or switches. A relay is usually mounted close to the device that requires the high current. Power is transferred directly from the battery source to the device through the relay.

A good example of how a relay is used would be the starter circuit on most V-twins. When you hit the starter button on the bars you're actually sending current from the button to the control side of the starter relay. Current passes through the coil in the control side of the relay to ground, creating a magnetic field as it does so. The magnetic field causes the contacts on the

load side of the relay to close. With these contacts closed, current moves from the battery to the starter solenoid (check the diagram). Without the relay the heavy wires needed to power the solenoid would have to run up to the switch in the handle bars. Note: Some of the new relays are solid state which eliminates the moving armature and the contacts described above though they do exactly the same job.

**Solenoids**

A solenoid used in a starter circuit is really nothing more than a specialized relay. In the case of a V-twin starter circuit, the solenoid is activated by the relay. Inside the solenoid are two coils of wire (a hold-in winding and a pull-in winding) with a movable plunger in the center. A copper disc is attached to one end of the solenoid. When the coils are energized, a magnetic field is created which causes the plunger to over-

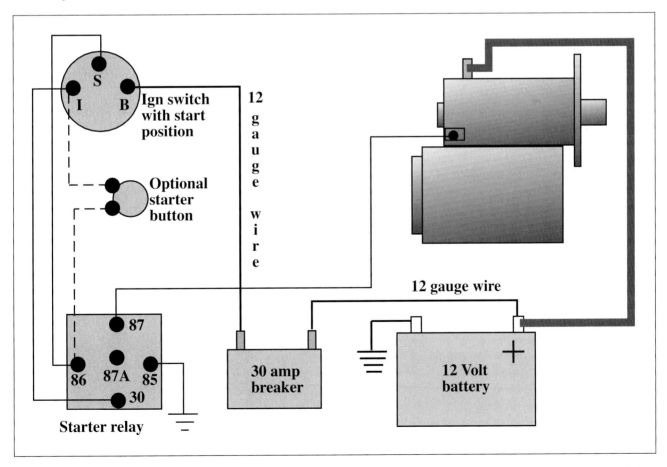

*The basic V-twin starter circuit. Terminal 30 could be wired hot all the time, but that way if the relay shorts out the bike will crank even with the ignition off. Wires not marked should be at least 16 gauge.*

come spring pressure and be drawn into the coils. As this happens the copper disc is brought into contact with two terminals inside the solenoid. One of these terminals is connected to the battery, the other connects to the starter motor. Once the copper disc makes the connection between the battery and the starter, current no longer flows to the pull-in winding and only the hold-in winding is used to hold the disc in place.

In addition to moving the copper disc up against the two larger terminals and thus acting as a switch between the battery and starter, the plunger also moves the starter pinion gear into mesh with the gear on the outside of the clutch basket.

## WHICH BATTERY TO BUY

The heart of your bike's electrical system is the battery. The battery is more than a power source and has three functions:

1. The battery produces electricity. The chemical reaction between the lead plates and the electrolyte, a water and sulfuric acid mix, creates electrical current. The voltage is determined by the number of cells.

2. The battery is also a storage device, able to store a large amount of current in its plates and capable of providing this current to the electrical system on demand.

3. In addition, the battery is a regulator of current in the system. As the engine rpm or system loads increase or decrease, the voltage and current flow go up and down. The battery acts as a buffer to damp out spikes and stabilize voltage in the system.

Batteries carry a number of ratings. The two most commonly used ratings for motorcycle batteries include cold cranking amps and amp hours. Cold cranking amps is perhaps the most common rating, and describes the amount of current the battery can provide for a certain length of time at a given temperature. To determine the rating a battery is chilled to zero degrees Fahrenheit and placed under a load in amps for 30 seconds while maintaining a voltage of 7.2 volts. The larger the rating number the more power that battery can put out to start your thumping big V-twin.

The amp-hour rating describes the number of hours a battery will withstand a certain amperage draw while holding the voltage above a minimum. When the catalogs list the "amp" rating, they are actually providing the amp-hour ratings provided by the battery manufacturer.

## BATTERY CONSTRUCTION

Like automotive batteries, most motorcycle batteries are constructed of positive and negative plates kept apart by separators,

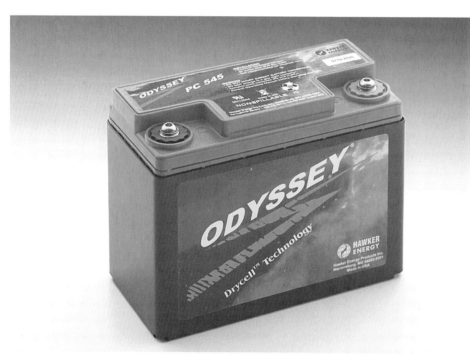

*Said to offer more power than any other batter of its size, the Odyssey batteries are not quite as tall, which means they fit in most oil tanks without the need for a recess in the seat pan. CCI*

grouped into cells, connected by straps and suspended in a solution of electrolyte. Each cell of the battery produces approximately two volts, by connecting six cells in series a 12 volt battery is created.

## SAFETY WARNING

Nearly all batteries emit hydrogen gas, explosive to say the least. Gassing is especially likely when the battery is being charged by an external charger or when the battery is under a load. For these reasons cigarettes, sparks and flames must be kept away from the battery. When jump starting be sure the last connection to be made is the negative cable, connected to the frame or engine of the bike being jumped. That way any spark will happen away from the battery.

Wrenches laid on the battery have the potential to short across the terminals and create an explosion. Also remember that metal jewelry conducts electricity at least as well as a wrench (silver and gold are both excellent conductors), which is one more reason to take off your watch and rings before you start work on the motorcycle. Remember too that batteries contain sulfuric acid, corrosive to metal and damaging to human skin. Spilled acid should be flushed immediately and thoroughly with water.

## BATTERY CHEMISTRY

The plates of the battery are made of lead alloys. These plates are suspended in a solution made up of sulfuric acid and water. When the battery discharges, sulfate (sulfur and oxygen) from the electrolyte combines with the lead on both the positive and negative plates.

As these sulfur compounds are bound to the lead plates oxygen is released from the positive plates. The oxygen mixes with hydrogen in the electrolyte to form water. As this reaction continues the acid becomes weaker and weaker, and more and more sulfate coats the plates. Charging the battery reverses the chemical process, forcing sulfates back into solution with the electrolyte and causing oxygen from the solution to move back onto the positive plate.

The down side to all this charging and discharging is the eventual flaking of lead particles from the plates which will diminish the battery's ability to produce and store energy. Further affecting battery performance is the fact that when a battery is left discharged, during the long winter lay up for example, the sulfates penetrate too deeply into the lead plates and cannot be driven back into solution. This is the condition that's often referred to as a "sulfated" battery.

Specific gravity is often used to check the state of charge for non-sealed batteries. Specific gravity simply measures the weight of a liquid as

*These are some of the more popular battery sizes, from older electric start Sportys (top left) to custom applications (bottom right). Most popular is the model on the top right, designed for early Softails and all FXRs (and thus the oil tank in most customs and choppers). CCI*

compared to water. The specific gravity of a fully charged battery ranges from 1.260 to 1.280 at 80 degrees Fahrenheit or 1.260 to 1.280 times as heavy as the same volume of water. As the battery becomes discharged the specific gravity drops because the electrolyte has a higher and higher percentage of water. This is also why a discharged battery will freeze on a cold winter's night while a fully charged battery will not.

Low and no-maintenance batteries change the chemical and physical construction of the plates slightly. By adding a chemical like calcium to the plates and changing the structure of the plates themselves, gassing of the battery is greatly reduced. This means a much smaller volume of corrosive/explosive gasses, little or no loss of water, and generally improved performance.

Recombination batteries, sometimes known under the name, valve-regulated, or Gas Recombinant Technology, go even further. These batteries contain all the "electrolyte" in a porous glass mat positioned between the cells. There is no liquid acid in batteries of this type and they can be mounted in nearly any position. Yuasa Battery says these recombinant batteries can be used in place of non-sealed batteries as long as the bike in question has a good charging circuit and a properly calibrated voltage regulator. All of which shouldn't be a problem as the bikes we are building here are essentially brand new. In most cases the new sealed batteries do offer better performance than their non-sealed cousins, both in terms of reduced self discharge and increased output for starting.

We can't close this battery section without mention of the Odyssey batteries. Relatively new, this is a starved-electrolyte design – meaning in short that there is no liquid electrolyte to leak out. These batteries can be mounted in nearly any position, and need no vent tube. Unlike some of the recombinant designs, these batteries are relatively insensitive to the input amperage (you are less likely to damage them by overcharging) and are said to offer "Cranking power that is double that of most wet acid batteries." If that's not enough, they have a two year shelf life and can be pulled down to zero volts hundreds of times without damaging the battery. The price is two or three times that of a good conventional battery, but the service life is estimated at three to eight years. Contact your local shop or click on their web site for more information.

### KEEP IT CHARGED FOR LONG LIFE

All batteries self discharge to some extent. This means a fully charged battery will draw itself down to zero voltage over time, even if the battery cables are removed. The answer is to recharge the battery when the bike sits for any extended period. For

*The only charger that can be left connected to the battery without any worry is the Battery Tender type chargers, available in this small maintenance model as well as higher output models.*

long battery life don't allow the battery to run down and don't let it sit for any length of time in a discharged condition.

When your motorcycle sits during those inevitable winter lay ups either make it a point to occasionally charge the battery or connect it to one of the "smart" battery chargers. The cheap little trickle chargers do not regulate the charge well enough to avoid damaging your battery when left connected too long. With this style of inexpensive charger, the rate of charge will diminish as the battery comes up to full charge, but the charge rate never tapers off enough to avoid battery melt down. The only chargers you can leave connected without the risk of damage to the battery are the "battery tender" type chargers.

Other tips for long life are mostly common sense. Keep the battery clean because a film of acid and dirt on the battery case will conduct a small current between the terminals, speeding self discharge. Higher temperatures increase the speed of self discharge, so be extra careful about charging the battery if the bike sits idle during the warm summer months.

Batteries for V-twins range in size from the rather small 12N7-4A, designed for kick-start bikes, to the huge HD-12 meant for older Dressers.

Most common among aftermarket and custom bikes is the "16" size battery. Available with different terminal positions and capacity ratings, this is the case size that matches up to the battery box supplied with most aftermarket frames. The 16-B is the standard battery in this group, the less common 16-LA uses the same case with the terminals reversed. Yuasa and others make a variety of batteries in this one case size.

Remember that the expensive high-torque starter can't crank to its full ability unless you provide it with an adequate power source. Even a hopped up 80 inch V-twin works the starter and battery pretty hard on a warm day. Considering all the money you're spending on this new bike, the cost of the battery is almost insignificant, so buy the best one you can. Many problems with hard starting, especially with big engines, can be corrected with the installation of a new, high capacity battery.

### INSTALL THE BATTERY

Most motorcycle frames provide only one spot to mount the battery. As vibration is hard on batteries, one of the cushions for sale in any of the catalogs is a good idea for the bottom of the battery box. If the battery has a vent tube it should be routed though the frame tubes to the area under the bike. If you want to be absolutely

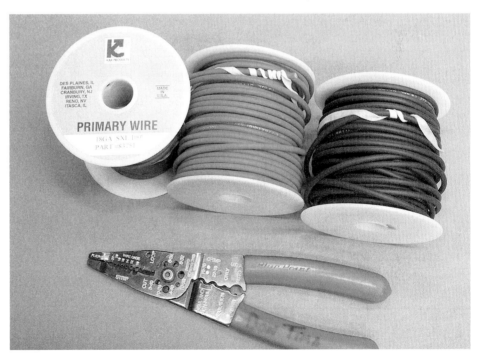

*Not all wire is created equal. This high quality wire uses "cross-linked polyurethane insulation" good for up to 284 degrees F before it melts. Vinyl insulation melts at about 170 degrees.*

*New generators are available for anyone who wants to run a real panhead or Knucklehead without the alternator left side case. These come with a 2 year warranty. Nifty solid state regulator is available as seen on the right. CSI*

sure the acid fumes won't attack the paint on the frame use one of the small plastic "overflow canisters" seen in many of the aftermarket catalogues and designed to prevent liquid acid from passing out the end of the vent tube. The other option is one of the totally sealed batteries already discussed which have no vent tube and will never need water.

Use at least the recommended six gauge cables between the battery and solenoid, from the solenoid to the starter and from the battery to ground. Smaller cable, as mentioned elsewhere, will prevent the battery's full potential from being delivered to the starter.

The ground cable must connect to the frame without the insulating affect of paint between the terminal and the frame itself. Some builders use a star washer between the terminal and the frame to ensure a good ground connection. Speaking of the insulating effect of paint, when the new frame is powder coated or painted be sure to mask off the part of the engine mount(s) where the motor actually sits. This will ensure a good ground connection between the frame and engine. With rubber-mount frames you need to run a separate ground cable from the engine to the frame because of the insulating effects of the rubber mounts.

Remember that if the insulation on the positive cable ever rubs through the frame you have a short lived but very intense arc welder. Use tie-wraps and rubber grommets to ensure that the cables can't be chafed through by sheet metal or the corner of a frame bracket. Another trouble spot is the wire that runs from the regulator back to the battery. This wire is hot at all times

*For anyone who wants the simplest of wiring harnesses, Compu-Fire offers this simple push switch for the back of the solenoid. Eliminates the starter switch and the relay. CSI*

and often unfused. If it rubs through the insulation at the front motor mount bracket for example it will destroy the regulator for sure and possibly the stator.

## STARTERS

The catalogs list late-model starter applications as either 1989 to 1993 or 1994 to present. Both of these are gear reduction starters, the difference in the two is one of the mounting bolts and the starter drive gear. Obviously the starter drive gears are different so they will correctly match with one of two possible ring gears used on the clutch shell. Much like getting all the primary parts matched, you need to be sure the starter is matched to the correct inner primary and clutch shell.

The average displacement of the engines installed in aftermarket V-twins is large and growing larger. The aftermarket has responded to this trend with bigger (as in higher-torque) starters. Which starter you install will depend on the engine you buy and the kind of advice you get from the local shops where you hang out. Though rated at only 1.2 KW, the factory starter is a high quality unit. Whether you buy from the dealership or not, be sure the starter you buy carries a brand name. As mentioned already, the best thing you can do to ensure enough grunt when you hit the button is to install a good battery, no matter which brand of starter you install.

Most aftermarket ignitions (the Crane HI-4 is one example) allow the engine to crank for one or two revolutions before the ignition fires which helps almost any V-twin achieve a higher cranking speed.

What was said earlier about using a heavier, rather than lighter, wire when in doubt applies doubly to the starting circuit. According to Don Tima, mechanic for Donnie Smith, "You have to be sure to run heavy enough wires to the load side of the starter relay. When wiring this side of the relay, from the main circuit breaker to terminal 30, and from terminal 87 to the solenoid, use 12 gauge wire, anything smaller will result in too much voltage drop in the circuit."

## CHARGING CIRCUITS

Though they look completely different, the alternator that resides under the primary cover of your new V-twin contains the same components as the one under the hood of your car or truck. Compared to an automotive application, most V-twin charging circuits are simplified, however. V-twin charging circuits are made up of three components: The stationary stator (the wires), the spinning rotor (the magnetic field) and the regulator.

Alternators, and generators too, make electricity by moving a wire through a field (or a

*V-twin charging circuits can be purchased as complete kits as shown here: The stator, the rotor and the matching regulator. CCI*

field over a wire) like they did in your 8<sup>th</sup> grade science class. Instead of one wire, the alternator stator in your bike is made up of many windings. And instead of moving the windings in the field, an alternator moves the field over a stationary stator.

In an automotive application, the magnetic field is created by running current through a coil of wire. By controlling the amount of current moving through the field winding the output of the alternator can be controlled. In a V-twin the field is made up of permanent magnets, so there is no easy way to control the output of the alternator. Extra output, more than is required to run the bike and charge the battery, is simply shunted to ground through the regulator. Considering that these are stripped bikes, many of which don't even have turn signals, it doesn't make a lot of sense to put on the high output alternator. All you need is enough power to recharge the battery, and run the lights and ignition.

Alternators and regulators are rated in amperage output. For scratch built custom bikes, the two logical choices are the 22 or the 32 amp system. By system we mean that the regulator, stator and stator cover (rotor) must be designed to work together – and that the plug on the stator must match the plug on the regulator.

The catalogs say that the 22 amp alternators were used by the factory from about 1981 to 1988 and that the 32 amp alternators were used from 1989 to 1999. While the 22 amp system probably has plenty of output for a stripped bike the parts are getting a little hard to come by. The default system for most current customs seems to be the 32 amp system with stator, stator cover (rotor) and regulator. Most of the aftermarket catalogs have various brand name charging circuit kits that include all the parts needed to assemble a complete charging circuit.

### A FEW FINAL NOTES:

Alternators produce alternating current (AC), which poses a problem as our motorcycles run on direct current (DC). Automotive alternators use two banks of diodes (one-way electrical valves) to convert the AC to DC. V-twin systems use the "regulator" for the conversion, which means the regulator actually has two jobs: to regulate the voltage output of the system *and* to rectify the current from AC to DC.

Some complete engines like those from Harley-Davidson, come with the stator and rotor already installed. Most of the engines you buy, however, will require that you buy a complete alternator assembly for the new motor.

Most regulators have three wires to connect, two go to the molded stator con-

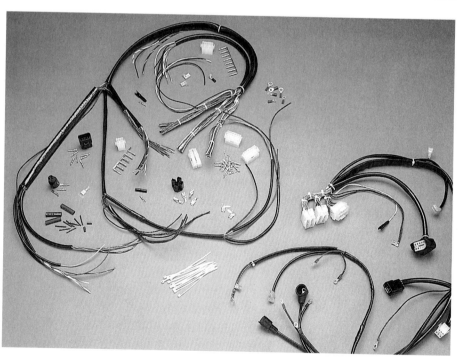

*These factory-type harness kits use stock terminal plugs, and come with the main harness, and the handle bar and taillight harnesses. Available longer than stock and with or without the terminals attached. CCI*

nection and one to the main circuit breaker or a positive battery connection. This means that the regulator itself grounds through its base so be sure there's no paint between that base and the frame bracket, or use a star washer between regulator and frame.

## BUY THE RIGHT STUFF: THE HARNESS AND SWITCHES

### The Wiring Harness

Not too long ago, most builders of custom bikes either bought a factory harness or made one from scratch. Today the catalogs are filled with complete harness kits, some of which emulate the factory harness while others take a simplified or high-tech approach to the topic of moving electricity from point A to point B. Professional bike building shops often make up a harness from scratch, often assembled using a sub-harness kit from one of the aftermarket suppliers so they get plenty of wires with the right color codes.

The factory has used the same color codes for years and it's a good idea, whether buying a complete harness or making one up from scratch, to stick with those codes to ease any trouble shooting that needs to be done down the road.

One of the problems of a stock-style harness is the bulk. Provisions for turn signals and all the other controls placed on the handle bars means lots of wires. So many that it's difficult to get the harness inside the frame, the preferred location for many custom bike builders. The other option is to build a harness from scratch, or have one built by the local custom bike building shop.

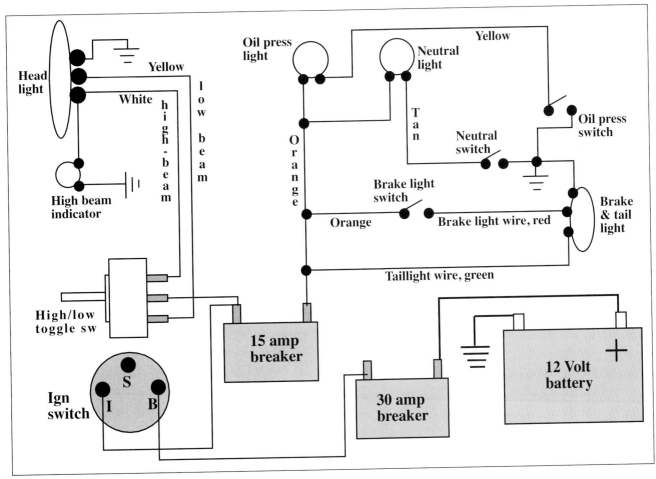

*Compliments of Don Tima, a simplified wiring diagram for a custom-type bike. Colors are those used in factory harnesses.*

As always, the aftermarket has responded to bike builders' needs for wiring harnesses. Pro-One and Thunder Heart are only two of the companies manufacturing complete harness kits. The Pro-One kits come in various configurations, one for Fat Bob tanks with the switch located on the dash, and three for bikes with the switch located on the left side. The differences in the three non-fat-bob harnesses center on whether or not handle-bar switches are used. Some of the new harness kits include a high tech controller in place of the old dash subassembly used with fat bob tanks, with its individual circuit breakers. These controllers come with integral relays and circuit breakers, and feature LEDs that indicate the condition of each circuit.

A number of professional shops still use the factory harnesses, either Softail or FXR-style, depending on the ignition switch location, for bikes that use handle bar switches and turn signals. When using the factory harness, most shops choose to use pre-1994 harnesses with the

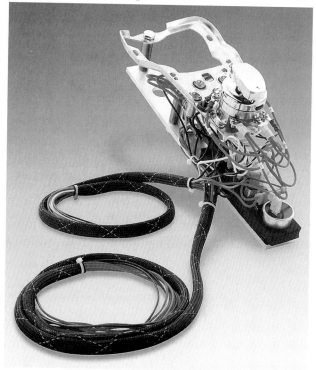

*From Pro-One comes this harness kit for bikes with flat-side fat bob tanks. Includes the ignition switch, circuit breakers and turn signal flasher. CCI*

non-waterproof connectors. A number of aftermarket companies offer what are essentially OEM-style harnesses in Softail and FXR style. Like the factory harnesses these come as a complete main harness, with plug-ins that connect to the handle-bar harness the taillight harness and so on.

Part of what makes the factory harnesses so complex is the handle bar switches. By placing all the switches on the coil or similar bracket, and eliminating the turn signals, the harness can be kept pretty simple. The factory uses a starter relay to feed current to the solenoid. The starter button closes the control circuit for the relay and the relay then sends power to the solenoid. Some builders like to use an automotive type switch with a spring loaded start position and eliminate the relay. Two potential problems arise however: First, the switch must be good enough to withstand the vibration and heat that it will be subject to in the coil bracket location. Second, by eliminating the relay you place a higher current load on the ignition switch, meaning again that it must be a high quality switch. To lighten the electrical load on the switch, some mechanics use a automotive type switch and leave the relay in the circuit between the ignition switch and the solenoid (check the illustrations).

If you decide the conventional harnesses are too massive and something simpler is in order, consider having a professional V-twin mechanic, one familiar with wiring projects, create and/or install the simplified harness. We've said this in the other books and it bears repeating: there is nothing that will give more trouble, usually at the worst possible time, than a poorly designed and installed wiring harness. Either use a good harness kit and install it very carefully, or ask for qualified help.

The rest of the switches you use should meet the same high quality standards as the ignition switch. Motorcycles subject all the switches to vibration, moisture and often heat. Switches are rated by the number of amps they can handle.

Don't buy the cute little sexy switches, buy the switches with enough heft and a high enough rating to do the job.

Most bikes use a hard-wired headlight. The only real switch in the circuit then is the high-low switch. You can use a factory-style switch located on the bars or a simple (single throw, double pull) "toggle" switch mounted on the coil bracket. Aftermarket switches are available in most catalogs or a Radio Shack store.

The connectors that connect the switch to the wiring and the rest of the harness should be soldered on, or at least well crimped. When two wires have to be joined, do it with a correctly soldered connection protected by heat shrink. There should be a law against the little squeeze together quick connectors, they often cut the wires as they make the connection and they provide a really good place for corrosion to start.

In closing the chapter on wiring we should repeat Don Tima's comments made for another book. Don strongly suggests you figure out where all the switches will go during the planning part of the building process, and whether or not any of them will be on the handle bars. If you're going to do a neat job of the wiring, especially if some of the wires go inside frame tubes, the wiring will have to be done as the bike goes together, not after everything else is finished.

Of note, the factory manuals contain detailed wiring diagrams for each model that can be very helpful when building a bike. In fact, blow-up manuals of nothing but wiring diagrams are available from your local dealer.

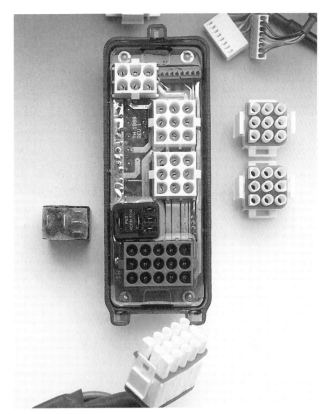

*This kit eliminates the circuit breakers and flasher, incorporates functions in one solid state module. Self-diagnosing, includes harness and all terminals. CCI*

*Designed by Dave Perewitz, this billet coil bracket with starter switch is designed to mount on the engine's left side and simplify the harness. CCI*

## Chapter Eight

# Sheet Metal

## Sportster Tanks & Trailer Fenders

Choppers might be the simplest of bikes, yet they still require sheet metal. At least a gas tank and minimalist rear fender. As with all other parts of our common obsession, there are more sheet metal choices now than ever before. The renaissance of the old world sheet metal forming skills means that now you even have a good chance to have one crafted by hand or modified to suit your unique needs.

**GAS TANKS**

Gas tanks fall into two major categories, one

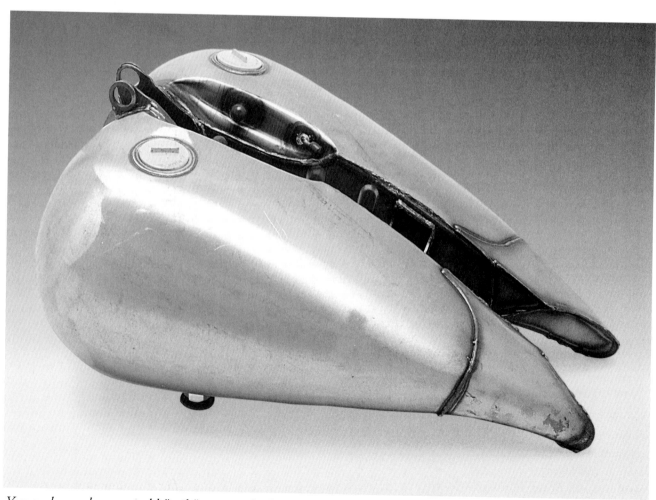

*You no longer have to weld "tails" on your fat bob tanks. These flat-sided fat bob tanks are designed by Dave Perewitz. Matching dash and appropriate seat are also available. Biker's Choice*

piece or two-piece tanks. The two-piece tanks, often called fat bob, come in what's know as "flat side" or solid mount. All modern two-piece tanks use the flat-sided design, meaning the tanks are rubber mounted. Earlier tanks, used prior to about 1984, bolted directly to the frame. This style has fallen from popularity, most currently offered two-piece tanks are of the flat-sided, rubber-mounted style.

Many frames come with, or can be ordered with, the tank mounts already in place. Mounts for flat side tanks are among the most popular. For raw frames that come without mounts, mounting kits are available from all the major aftermarket companies, to aid you in attaching the tank(s) to most frames.

For years the classic two-piece gas tanks came in three and a half, or five gallon sizes. Those two sizes are still available, as are some six gallon sizes from Custom Chrome and Chrome Specialties to name only two. Stretched versions of the tried and true fat bob tank are also available in various capacities, some with flush-mount gas caps. Extension panels, designed to be welded on to the ass-end of each tank, are also available from Milwaukee Iron to name only one supplier.

The classic chopper of old carried a Sportster, Mustang or "peanut" tank. Today, all those shapes are as popular as ever. Sportster tanks, either the little two and a half gallon variety, or the larger "king" tanks can be purchased from the local dealership, (most Harley-Davidson sheet metal is of very high quality) or in your local aftermarket shop. The dealers offer two versions of the Sporty tank, the

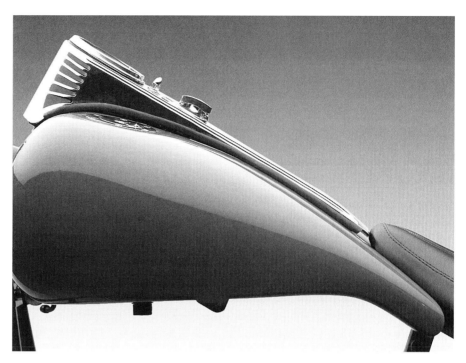

*Stretched tanks are not all created equal. Pick a size and shape that best fits your design ideas for the bike. Pictured are stretched tanks available in 3-1/2 to 7 gallon volumes. Can be ordered for screw-in or aircraft type caps. CCI*

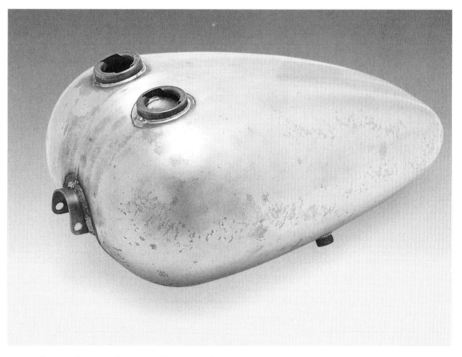

*For the traditionalists in the crowd Paughco offers Mustang tanks in various configurations from 5 gallon with a deep tunnel, to 2 gallon with a shallow tunnel to put the tank up on top of the tube. Biker's Choice*

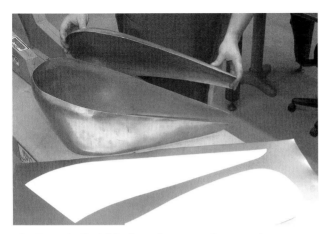

*At Donnie Smith's shop they sometimes make gas tanks by hand. This partially completed example, is the work of resident tin man Rob Roehl.*

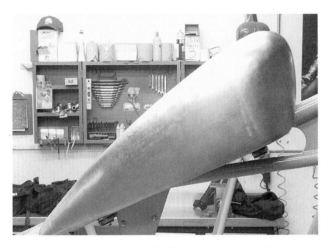

*Rob often shapes the tanks from .050 inch aluminum killed or "draw" steel, available from better metal yards.*

*To mount the tanks Rob has Johnny Galvin, in-house machinist, turn out these plugs which he then welds into the bottom of the tank.*

older tanks with the hard bottom edge, and the newer style with the same basic shape but with softer, rounded edges. Custom Chrome offers a "Sportster" tank with a nearly flat bottom, so the tank sits up on top of the frame for that period-correct chopper profile.

Making a tank from scratch is a difficult task. At best there are only a handful of shops and fabricators capable of forming a truly scratch built tank. The complex curves that make up most gas tanks requires shrinking and stretching skills of the highest order. To avoid having to form complex curves, early fabricators made chopper tanks from what were essentially flat panels. Often known as "coffin tanks" these vessels for petroleum might look rather crude today, but they are just right for certain early-style choppers.

You might think that having one of these made is relatively simple, given the flat panels that make up most of these tanks. There's still a lot of cutting and welding involved however. The good news is you don't have to make, or have one fabricated. Independent Gas Tank Company already fabricates at least one style of coffin tank, available in various dimensions, to fit the chopper of your dreams.

The renaissance of choppers has helped give birth to a number of small shops staffed by passionate builders and fabricators. Dedicated to nothing but choppers, many of these small shops are bringing to market frame and sheet metal designs that range all over the map in terms of styles.

Custom Cycle Creations offers traditional Sporty type tanks with a nearly flat bottom, as well as what they call their traditionally styled tanks with more of a teardrop shape that comes back into a sharp point.

From the shop of Cyril Huze comes what he calls New School designs. One example is his slender hot chop gas tank available in 3 or 5 inch stretch. A perfect match for one of his Fat Katz Chopper frames.

Most of the one-piece tanks, whether in a Sporty shape or a long narrow spear, don't come with mounting kits. Some of the tanks do have bungs on the bottom that are tapped for a standard 5/16 or 3/8 inch bolt. This still leaves you needing a means of attaching some kind of appropriate brackets to the frame.

At Donnie Smith's shop outside Minneapolis, Rob Roehl welds bungs into the bottom of his fabricated tanks. These bungs are fabricated in house by John Galvin, resident machinist. "Sometimes we recess the bungs into the tank," explains Rob, "to create a tank with a smooth bottom. But usually we just have them flush mounted into the bottom of the tank." With larger tanks Rob often reinforces the area around the bung so the tank has more support.

The tabs on the frame that locate the tank are made from flat one-inch wide mild steel strap. Each is cut to the right length and then drilled to the correct size to accept the rubber cushions used for flat-side gas tanks. The nearby photos probably do a better job of explaining Rob's mounting system than all the words in the world.

When designing the mounting system for your tanks, remember that when full, the tank(s) is quite heavy, and subject to that old V-twin bugaboo – vibration. When possible, stick with the factory mounts, they work. Professional shops sometimes move the upper front mount, on a set of typical fat bob tanks, down between the tanks (check the photo on page 82). In this way they keep most of the factory's rubber mounting system but make it possible to run a slim dash that follows the contour of the tank.

For all the reasons already stated, brackets mounted to the tank must be well supported and welded on by someone who knows how to make a strong, non-brittle weld. For more about mounting tanks, see the assembly sequences at the back of the book.

## FENDERS: DESIGN AND MOUNTING TIPS

Even if you're only running one fender, it needs to be chosen and mounted with care. You can have a rolled fender, like those from Jesse James, Russ Wernimont or a more traditional fender with skirts. "Trailer" fenders are still available for that very traditional hardtail look.

Rear fenders mounted to a soft-tail type chassis need to be supported by struts. If you want the new bike really clean, then you can buy strut-less fenders like the ones offered for sale by Milwaukee Iron (and others). Strut-less rear fenders are made from heavy gauge steel and/or hide a support strut up inside the fender on either side.

To create a soft-tail with more of the hardtail illusion, the rear fender can be mounted to the swingarm instead of the frame. In this way the fender can be mounted down close to the tire. The down side is the fact that you can only use a solo seat, or a two piece seat, because the rear of the seat is going to move with the fender and wheel.

Mounting the fender down close to the tire is

something everyone strives for. It tends to lower the whole machine in a visual sense and helps the bike look way cool. The tire-hugging-fender routine can be overdone of course. More than one professional builder has been forced to remove a fender after the first road test or after the bike was ridden hard the first time, to replace or repaint the fender. Note the comments made in Chapter Four.

If the bike you're building is not part of a rolling chassis kit, then you need to spend considerable time during the mock up period making sure the fender shape is the one that best fits the bike. With the frame sitting at ride height it's a good idea to try the fenders in more than one position. If things just don't look right try another fender. When viewing the bike from the side, make sure the inner radius of the fender lines up with the edge of the rim.

On bikes with rear suspension, the rear fender must be mounted so it can't touch the tire even when the suspension hits the bottom of travel. The suspension should be run from full extension to full compression with the fender in place so you know the tire

*This is a look at one of Rob's finished tanks from the bottom. Bigger tanks have the area around the weld-in plug reinforced.*

101

can't hit the fender or the mounting hardware. Bolts used under the fender should point away from the tire so that if you bottom the suspension especially hard the tire won't be ripped up by the threads on the bolt that mounts the fender or seat. Ny-lock type locking nuts are a good idea, especially if the fenders are glass or plastic, where you don't want to super tighten the bolts. Remember that a fender that shakes loose and drops onto the tire will likely lock up the tire.

## INTERVIEW, DONNIE SMITH

*The best way to introduce Donnie Smith (though for most enthusiasts he doesn't need an introduction) might be to explain that Donnie is building choppers - again. Donnie you see was building choppers when they were originally discovered. In fact, Donnie Smith was part of the very successful Smith Brothers and Fetrow chopper shop that operated in Minneapolis from 1971 to 1985. During that time they designed and fabricated many of their own parts, including a girder fork assembly, and built plenty of show-winning choppers. Today Donnie runs Donnie Smith Custom Cycles in Blaine,*

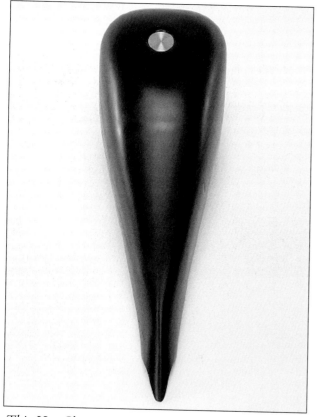

*This Hot Chop gas tank from Cyril Huze is available standard or stretched, a good example of the new tank shapes showing up on new choppers.*

*where they turn out everything from custom baggers to high class choppers.*

*Donnie, how does a person match the kind of bike they want with one of the many frames on the market?*

The kind of bike you want to build is probably based on something you saw in a magazine and most of the time the magazine gives you the information as far as the brand is concerned. If the magazine doesn't give the brand and the dimensions any good shop should be able to tell from the photos what the rake and stretch dimensions are.

*What about the tubing that frames are made of, do people need chrome moly for the typical motorcycle frame or is mild steel better?*

I don't think you need the 'moly for these frames. Weight isn't an issue on these bikes and I don't prefer it.

*Donnie, can you want to talk about the relative merits of the different types of forks; hydraulic, springers and girders?*

The telescopic fork is simpler to manufacture, it's more state of the art. It used to be that Indians came with a girder and Harleys had a springer What I like about a girder, over the springer, is the installation of fender and brakes. You don't have to worry about windup with a girder. And the fender doesn't move up and down as the bike goes over bumps, like it does on a springer. You don't need that linkage that the new Harleys have to maintain the fender position relative to the tire as the bike goes over bumps.

In the old days the springers came with no shocks. We adjusted the top springs so they were under tension and that tended to dampen the main springs. But the girder with a shock had real damping in both directions. I'm more in favor of the girder, they ride better, the brake and fender don't move. We designed one for Chrome Specialties and it will be in their catalog.

I like girders but the springer will hold it's own forever. The new ones do have shocks and there are kits from Star West to add shocks to some others. For some people a springer is part of the Harley look.

*Once a person has a frame, is there any easy way to figure out how long the front end, or the tubes, should be?*

You almost have to do a mock up of the whole bike to get it done.

*What about trail, do you have any recommended guidelines for trail?*

Four to six inches of trail should work pretty well. Too short, less than 4 inches, and they're squirrely at speed. Too much, over 6 inches, and they get heavy at slow speeds. This is what I like in my regular street bikes.

*What about choosing wheels and tires, any recommendations?*

People should pick the frame first, to make sure how big a rear tire will fit, then they can choose the rear tire and rim. I personally like a 200X16 inch instead of an 180X18, that's my personal preference. That skinny little sidewall on the 250X18 and some of the other new tires just doesn't look right to me.

*How about brakes, Is there a typical brake set up you use in your shop?*

We run a lot of four piston, dual caliper brakes up front. A four piston caliper is plenty of brake. You could also run two little two-piston calipers on the front, it would reduce the weight. And with the big rear tire and the weight on the rear of the bike the front brakes aren't quite as important.

*What are the mistakes people make when they build a chopper, or any scratch-built bike for that matter?*

They don't ask enough questions, or they use the wrong combination of parts. And they do sloppy work.

People buy a frame 'cause it's a good deal. I tell them, 'you pay for what you get.' Recently some guy bought a cheap frame, after I quoted him a price for a good frame, and the tank mounts were way off. So now he brings it to us to fix. He told me, 'You kind of knew this was going to happen though didn't you.'

When you look at the overall project you might save a few thousand dollars if you buy a cheap frame but you spend twice that making everything work and fit. And after all that trouble you're probably not happy with the end result. The frame is so important to the whole project, it's one place people shouldn't try to save money. You can pay now or pay later.

*An interesting group of new fender shapes are available from Milwaukee Iron including some with a lot of motion in the design. Available to fit narrow and wide-glide forks. CCI*

*These traditional fenders are intended for rigid frames and come in widths that range from 7-1/2 to 9 inches to cover even the fattest tires. CCI*

# Chapter Nine

# Plumbing & Hardware

## Dash-Two Hoses & Grade 8 Bolts

The importance of plumbing and hardware can't be overstated. For both safety and aesthetics, the hoses that carry fluids and the bolts that hold the bike together are as important as that 120 inch motor. The original idea was to create a short side-bar on hoses and hardware for the Chassis chapter. But the side-bar grew and grew until it became a chapter of its own – the one you find here.

### BRAKE HOSES

Connecting the master cylinder(s) to the calipers

*Call it hardware or call it jewelry, the importance of hoses and clamps and fasteners can't be overstated. If you stop and think about it, a motorcycle, especially a hand-built custom motorcycle, is nothing more than a collection of hardware.*

are the flexible brake lines. Because the hydraulic pressure in the brake system approaches 1000psi you can only use hoses approved for use in hydraulic brake systems. When buying hydraulic hoses many builders use braided stainless lines from companies like Russell, Goodridge or Accel. The braided lines use Teflon inner liners to actually carry the fluid. Unlike the OEM style hoses, which may swell just slightly with brake application, the Teflon liners do not expand even a little under hard braking and thus provide a solid, linear feel to the brakes.

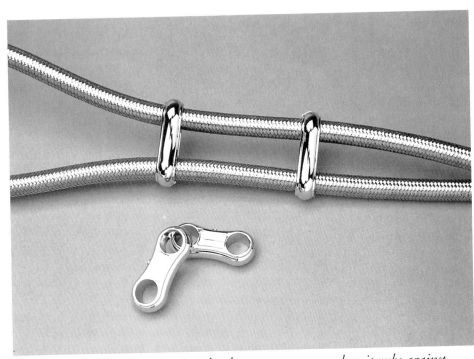

*Stainless hose acts as a saw when it rubs against almost anything, meaning that whether it's brake line or oil line it needs to be well clamped. These very clean little clamps are from the Arlen Ness collection and are available in various sizes and configurations.*

Both Russell, Goodridge and others provide a variety of stainless hose styles. Most common are the universal hoses available in various lengths with a female connector attached at either end. By combining the universal hose with the right banjo bolt and connector on either end it's possible to find the right combination of hose and ends for nearly any imaginable application.

Even among the universal hoses there are differences. Notably, some hoses are DOT approved, which might be a factor in states with tough inspection laws. Other differences include diameter, which comes in three sizes known as dash 2, 3 and 4, with 2 being the smallest and 3 the most common by far.

To explain the unusual designations used for braided hoses requires a short digression: Much of this high-end hose market started as surplus from the military, and thus

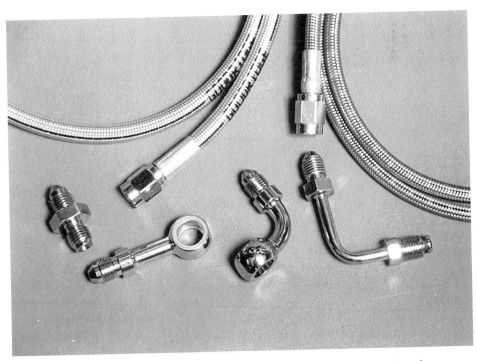

*Stainless brake lines come with or without the plastic sheathing. These hoses from Goodridge match up to flare and banjo fittings to fit almost any application.*

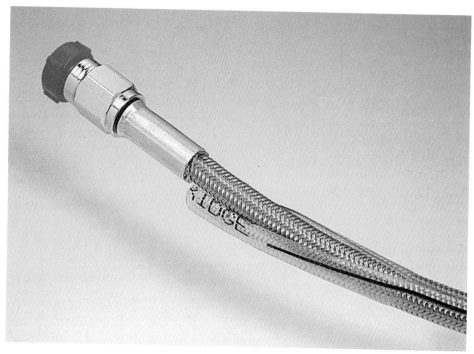

*Though it will discolor over time the wrapped stainless will not cut into the paint or other hoses and won't create a short if it comes into contact with a hot terminal.*

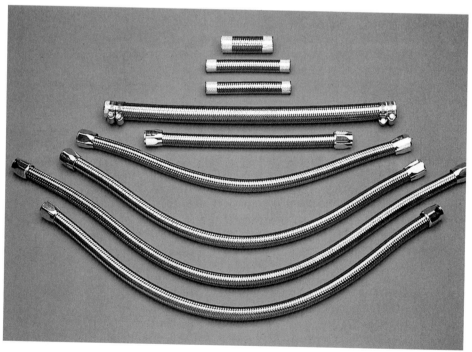

*These oil line kits from Russell come in the right lengths for most soft-tail type bikes. Ness*

uses what is commonly called the AN (Air Corps/Navy) measuring system. Fittings are all 37 degree instead of the more common 45 degree used in most American OEM situations. In this system, hose sizes are often indicated by one or two digits.

What's called a "dash three" is generally written -03, or simply, -3. The three is the numerator of a fraction with 16 as the denominator. So the dash three equals 3/16 inch. It gets a little confusing because the 3/16 doesn't indicate the exact I.D. or even the O.D. At the time of implementation each size was designed to replace an existing hard-metal line with a flexible line of about the same I.D. Thus a dash three has about the same I.D. as a standard 3/16 inch brake line. A dash four (-04) has the same internal diameter as a 4/16, or 1/4 inch steel line.

If you want pre-made hoses without the additional hardware of a universal hose, some aftermarket shops stock hoses for common lengths and applications, or you can call a company like Performance Machine or Goodridge (some shops also have this capacity) with your specifications and they can make up a hose from scratch. Accel has a new line of hoses with ends attached, that utilize chrome plated ends for maximum visual appeal.

Goodridge makes a hose with a clear outer cover so the stainless braid won't act like a saw if it rubs against the fender. Or you can buy shrink tubing for brake hoses and use it to coat all or part of your new stainless brake lines. The best way to ensure that the new hose won't act like a saw against that candy paint job is to route it correctly and clamp it securely.

The threads and fittings used for brake lines and banjo bolts are not as standardized as the threads used on common bolts and nuts. For this reason be sure you use matching components - a Russell end on a Russell hose.

## OIL LINES

The hose used for oil lines is often rated for fuel as well. The least expensive oil lines are black neoprene hose with at least one internal layer of rayon or nylon to give the hose extra strength. Many of these come molded to fit specific applications. For a new scratch-built bike however, many people want braided stainless hose.

The trouble with "braided stainless" is the fact the quality varies greatly. High quality stainless braided hose is available from companies like Aeroquip or Earl's in at least three different quality levels. To pick just one example, Earl's makes an Auto-flex hose made up of a single synthetic inner layer, wrapped in a bonded fabric weave, that is then wrapped in braided stainless. In the case of most premium hoses, the stainless braid is bonded to the inner liner, or wrapped so tightly that it actually adds to the burst strength of the hose. With less expensive non-brand-name hose the stainless braid is simply slid over what is basically a standard Neoprene hose, the stainless is only adding to the abrasion resistance and the appearance of the hose.

In the case of both Earl's and Aeroquip, they offer bright anodized ends matched to their various hoses. John Reed, designer for Custom Chrome, likes to use the high quality hose and

explains, "When I build a bike I like to plumb it by hand, that way I get the hoses the exact length that I want. I use the hose from Aeroquip and their ends, by the time I'm through I've got little pieces of stainless embedded in the ends of my fingers but the job is really neat. This also allows you to make nice little brackets, run the hose through the bracket, and then put the end on later."

For anyone who doesn't want to go to the local auto parts store where they sell bulk high quality hose and the matching ends, all the major aftermarket catalogs are filled with braided-stainless oil hose kits for the most popular bikes. Even for a chopper (as long as the engine and oil tank are in conventional locations) you may be able to find a kit with pre-cut hoses designed for a rigid frame.

The best of these hose kits come with chrome plated fittings already crimped onto the hose ends. Some offer a clear hose covering the stainless. You can also buy bulk "stainless" hose at most shops, cut it to length and then use an "econo clamp" (which is just a deluxe version of a standard hose clamp) to secure the ends.

The comments made regarding stainless hose used for brake line bear repeating. Though the wrap provides resistance to abrasion, the stainless is aggres-

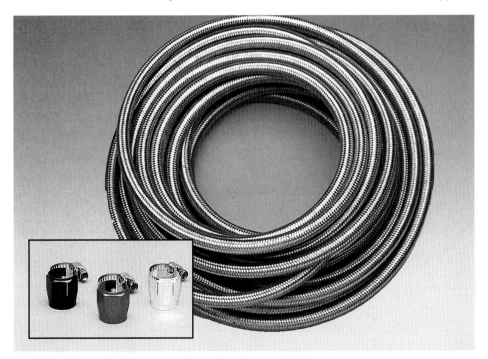

*Hose in the right size for oil lines is available bulk from Russell and can be clamped in a variety of ways including the small clamps shown. Ness*

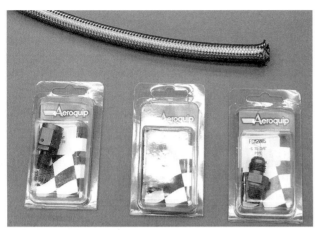

*Our little hose fabrication how-to project starts with Aeroquip AQP hose and the appropriate compression-style fittings.*

*Under the outer braid is a smooth elastomer hose with bonded stainless reinforcing. This hose is resistant to all standard fuels and lubricants and is good to 1000 psi.*

*Each company makes a range of fittings, it's a good idea to use hose and fittings from the same company.*

sive if it contacts anything else, including other hoses. Being metal, the wrap will conduct electricity, should it come between a hot terminal and ground. Again, the best way to prevent any of these little problems is with careful layout and plenty of brackets.

## THE BASIC BOLT

A bolt is nothing more than a threaded fastener designed to screw into a hole or nut with matching female threads. In order to proceed with the discussion, we need to get a little nomenclature out of the way first. Technically a bolt is a fastener without a washer face under the head, while a capscrew has a washer face under the head.

More terms. The minor diameter of a bolt or capscrew is the diameter measured at the smallest point, the bottom of the threads on either side. The major diameter is the diameter measured at the largest point, the tops of the threads on either side. The shank is the unthreaded part of the bolt's shaft, the bearing surface is the raised and polished portion just under the head of a quality capscrew. The length is measured from the lower edge of the bearing surface, or the bottom of the head, to the end of the bolt. The grip length is the length of the unthreaded portion while the thread length is simply the length of the threaded portion of the bolt. Peak and root describe the point and the notch of a thread when viewed in cross-section.

## BOLT MANUFACTURE

Most quality bolts are made in a rolling or forming operation. The raw stock, known as "wire," is rolled through special dies that form the threads without any cutting. Though at first this might seem the wrong way to make a bolt the reasons bolts are made in this way are numerous and hard to refute.

First, cutting threads is very time consuming. Second, cutting leaves rough edges behind, even the sharpest tooling will leave small tears in the surface of the metal. Third, cutting threads means cutting across the grain of the bolt, making it much weaker. Rolling threads on the other hand encourages the grain to flow with the threads. Rolling the threads also compresses or forges the surface of the threads making them much stronger. A quality thread-rolling operation leaves a smooth polished surface.

## THREADS

The earliest threads were not rolled however, they were cut on lathes. These were the first "regu-

The project takes place at the shop of Neal Letourneau where the first job is to wrap the hose in electrical tape and cut it with a zinger.

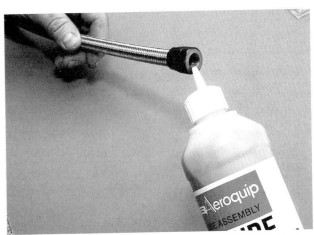

Lubricant (30w oil can be used as well) will aid the insertion of the remaining part of the fitting called the nipple.

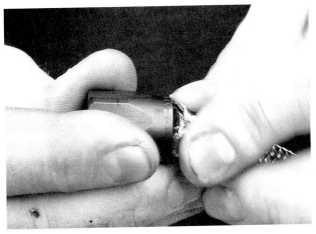

In Neal's hand is part of the fitting called the socket.

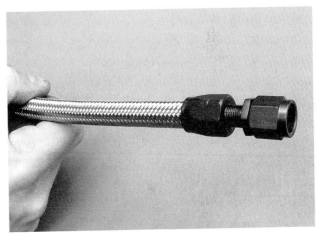

The nipple is started into the socket by hand....

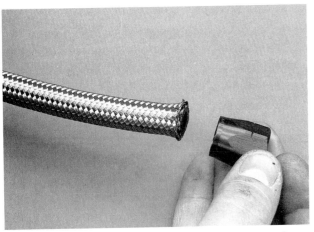

The idea is to slide the hose past the edge and up into the socket - sometimes easier said than done.

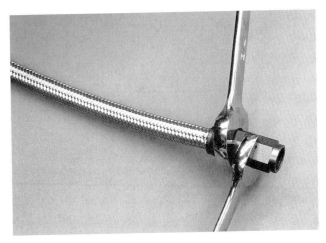

... then screwed into the socket until the gap between the two is about a thumbnail wide.

lar" fasteners with a specified pitch, thread profile, and diameter. Bolts that could be replaced with an identical part. Until the advent of standardized bolts you couldn't just run down to the hardware store to buy a new 5/16 UNC bolt to replace the one that fell out of your cotton gin.

Early engineers needed a way to describe each and every bolt. They developed a nomenclature to precisely describe the size and shape of any thread. Today we use pretty much the same terms to describe the threads on a bolt or capscrew that they did. Though a few of the basic terms were covered already, there are just a few more to consider.

- The pitch is the distance from one thread crest to another.
- The thread angle is the angle of the threads when viewed in cross-section.
- The root is the base of the thread, or the "notch" at the bottom of two adjacent flanks.
- The crest of the thread is the very top of each thread, the opposite of the root so to speak.

Despite this supposedly standardized nomenclature, there are different ways of describing the threads on a bolt or capscrew, depending on whether it's an "American" or metric part.

While American or unified bolts are described as having 24 or 18 threads per inch, the metric system describes a bolt as having a pitch of a certain dimension, like 1.0 mm.

## GRADING SYSTEMS AND SPECIFICATIONS
### Thread Specifications in the Real World.

What we often call NC and NF or national course and national fine, are actually UNC and UNF. Or unified national course and unified national fine. This system came out of the confusion that arose during WWII when English mechanics tried to repair American Airplanes with Whitworth nuts and bolts. The ensuing troubles convinced the allies that they needed some type of unified thread form. The "unified" system they settled on retained most of the then-current American standards and specifications.

The specifications called for an included angle of 60 degrees for both the coarse and fine threaded fasteners, all of which were measured in the well known inch system.

There has been some evolution of the thread specifications since those first specifications were written, but most of those have to do with the radius at the base of the thread. A sharp V-shaped notch at the base of the threads makes an ideal stress riser - a spot where the bolt is likely to fatigue and break.

Even a flattened V includes two smaller notches, which again make ideal spots for the concentration of stress.

Because the original specifications for unified threads allowed for a flattened V, there was enough room in those specifications for a improvement in the shape of the threads. Years earlier, engineers discovered that they could extend the fatigue life of a fastener considerably by simply "rounding" the root, or base of the threads. Obviously this rounding, specified as a particular radius, eliminated the stress risers found in a pure V or flattened V shape. Most of the better bolts and cap-

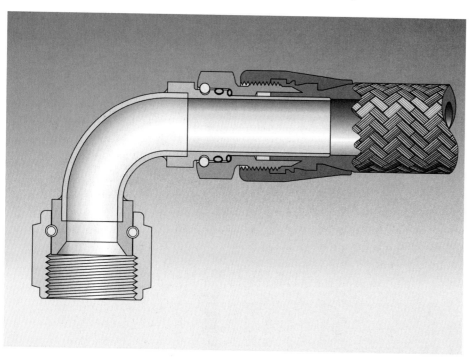

*High quality hose ends can be roughly categorized as either compression or cutter style. Shown is a cutter style hose end, note how the fiting actually cuts into the hose itself. Earl's*

screws (including SAE Grade 8) now specify a "R" thread which simply spells out the specific radius at the bottom of the thread.

## THE SAE GRADING SYSTEM

As bike builders and shade-tree mechanics, most of us are familiar with SAE graded fasteners. These are the well-known Grade 5 and Grade 8 bolts we get from Gardner Wescott, the local industrial supply house or the local hardware store.

SAE bolts come in various strengths. These bolts carry the radial dashes on the head that most of us have learned to identify. Three dashes is a Grade 5 while six identify the bolt as a Grade 8, a bolt many of us consider "as good as it gets."

Bolts are measured in pounds per square inch of tension or stress. The ultimate tensile strength or UTS is the point at which the bolt breaks. The other specification given for quality bolts is the yield point, or point at which the bolt will no longer bounce back to its original dimension once the stress is removed.

An SAE Grade 2 bolt, often called a hardware-store bolt, is rated at 74,000 psi UTS up to a size of 3/4 inch. This same bolt has a yield strength of 57,000 psi.

Moving up the scale, a Grade 5 bolt, the point at which good bolts start, is rated at 120,000 psi UTS and has a published yield point of 92,000 psi. Grade 5 bolts are considered good enough for most general purpose automotive and motorcycle use. What many of us consider the ultimate bolt, the Grade 8 bolt, is rated at 150,000 psi and 130,000 psi yield strength. Properly manufactured Grade 8 fasteners use the "R" thread root to minimize the effects of fatigue.

Quality Grade 5 and 8 bolts have a manufacturer's marking on the head along with the radial dashes. This makes it easier to trace the

bolt back to the manufacturer. Something like 'LE' for Lake Erie. Grade 2 bolts do not need dashes and do not need a manufacturer's mark. The manufacturer's mark makes manufacturers accountable and increases the likelihood that the bolt you buy is the bolt you think it is.

## OH NUTS

The best bolt in the world isn't worth a damn without matching female threads. Those threads commonly take the form of a nut, or threads tapped into a casting. In the case of a capscrew and nut, the strongest union is provided if the male and female components have fine threads (all other factors being equal), because this way you get a larger root diameter, and there is more physical contact between the threads.

The threads cut into a casting are often coarse, as coarse threads are better suited to those "coarse" materials and help to compensate for the difference in strength between the material the bolt is manufactured from and the material the casting is made from.

Nuts break down into those that are self-locking and those considered free-running. True experts in the field tend to give little consideration to free-run-

*Though it might seem like overkill for a small shop, the master Allen bolt assortment would probably prevent enough parts chasing to pay for itself in gas savings alone. Biker's Choice.*

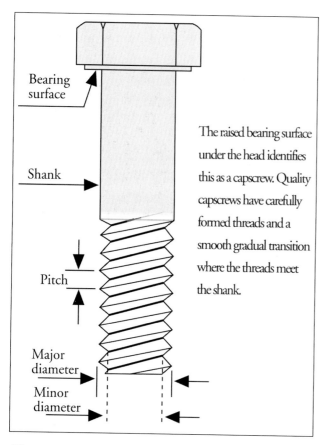

Bearing surface

Shank

Pitch

Major diameter

Minor diameter

The raised bearing surface under the head identifies this as a capscrew. Quality capscrews have carefully formed threads and a smooth gradual transition where the threads meet the shank.

*The major parts of a quality capscrew.*

*The head of the bolt tells the story: Six radial dashes indicates a Grade 8 while three indicates a Grade 5. Quality bolts and capscrews should have a logo (called the manufacturer's headmark) so it can be traced back to the manufacturer. Avoid bolts that don't have a headmark.*

ning nuts. Generally there isn't a good reason not to use a good self-locking nut. These self locking nuts are especially helpful when screwing on semi-fragile parts, like fiberglass fenders, where you don't want the bolts terribly tight for fear of cracking the 'glass.

## SELF-LOCKING NUTS

More commonly used than a jam nut to ensure the nut and bolt don't come "undone" self-locking nuts are available in a variety of styles. One of the most common is the ny-lock type of lock-nut that combines a six-point nut with a nylon collar. Nylock is a trade name, so maybe it's better to term these nylon-collar nuts. In any case, the nylon collar has no threads, so as the nut is screwed onto the bolt the bolt threads must force (but not cut) their way through the collar, which is sized to have an I.D. slightly smaller than the major diameter of the bolt. As the bolt threads its way through the nylon, friction is created between the metal male and female threads. Added to this is the friction between the nylon collar and the bolt threads. The combination works well and resists vibration as well as anything else.

Nylon-collar nuts are available in chrome and stainless and can be reused. What these lock-nuts aren't good at is enduring high heat situations. For securing exhaust flanges and the like, a better choice is an all-metal lock nut.

## A LITTLE HEAD...

### ALLEN BOLTS

Universally known as "Allen" bolts, (Allen is another trade name) these Socket Headed Cap Screws are the preferred fastener for many bikers. The small head can be an advantage in many situations and these fasteners are reputed to be extremely durable, but most people use them for their apparent precision and that intangible feel of quality they lend to anything they touch.

Most bolt catalogs state the all SHCS bolts are at least 170,000 psi for UTS. In other words, better than a Grade 8 bolt. Unfortunately, this is no longer true. Like all the other hardware you buy, you now have to be careful where, and from whom, you buy your SHCS bolts. In particular, the chrome plated variety are often only about a Grade 5, but you don't know unless you ask. The other problem that comes along with these nifty fasteners is the relatively long threads, which may have to be shortened with a die-grinder or hacksaw.

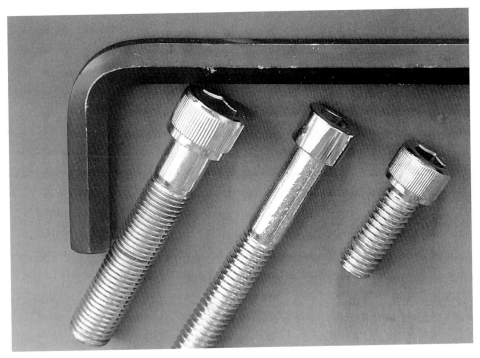

*Chrome plated socket headed cap screws come in both smooth and knurled heads.*

The small head, which many see as an advantage, can be a problem as well. The small size means it's hard to use the full strength of the bolt to clamp things together. And if you use a standard stamped washer under the head it will deform later leaving you with a loose bolt. The answer is to use a hardened and ground washer under the head of the SHCS bolt.

The only thing better than an SHCS is one with a button head. These little rounded heads look like rivets. The button head however, allows for only a very shallow female socket, meaning you can't get a good grip with the wrench. So don't use the button heads when you need serious clamping pressure.

## CHROME BOLTS

They say chrome is king, but when it comes to a chrome plated bolt, there are a few things you should know. First, chrome plating a bolt weakens it slightly. Compensation may be provided if the manufacturer started with a high quality bolt. The other problem is the

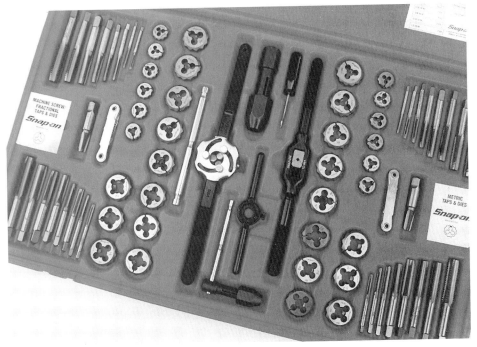

*Every good tool box should include a set of taps and dies, for cleaning threads on critical bolts and tapping that occasional hole in a non-critical application.*

fact that these bolts have no marking on the head, so there is no easy way to judge their quality. For this reason it's extra important that you purchase the bolts from a supplier you trust to provide good quality fasteners.

You can have your own bolts chrome plated, but considering the availability of already-chromed bolts, it's not a good trade off. While the nickel and chrome plating aren't very thick, the process does add to the dimensions of the threads, meaning that shiny bolt you

*A good capscrew has a raised bearing surface just under the head.*

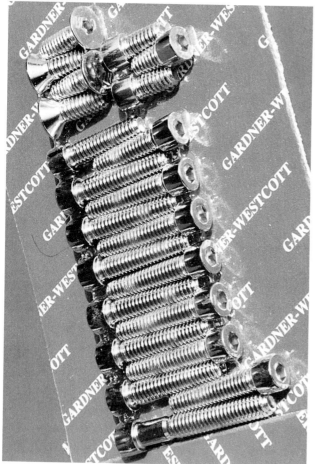

*Gardner-Wescott makes a variety of decorative kits designed to fit one particular application.*

just had plated might stick when it goes into the hole (or more likely, when you try to screw it out). If you do have a bolt chrome plated, be sure to mask off the threads so they don't grow in size.

If in doubt about any bolt or nut, it's a good idea to chase the threads with a tap or die. If the die or tap is doing much cutting, there's a problem and the best approach is to look for a replacement.

The use of chrome plated SHCS can be filled with frustration. Anyone who has used these bolts soon discovers that rust often develops down inside the head, due to the fact that the chrome plating process just can't get plating down into those crevices. The answer is to use the little chrome caps that snap into the socket, paint the inside of the heads, or put a dab of clear silicon on the end of the wrench the first time the bolt is used.

Because the chrome can flake off the fastener, even a good one, and cause it to bind in the hole, a good anti seize should be used on chrome bolts. Loctite products also do a good job of preventing metal to metal contact and can also be used to prevent galling of chrome nuts and bolts. Most of these bolts are Grade 5 or Grade 8, which means you want to be sure they don't gall and break off in the hole.

Because they're so tough, they're also hard as hell to drill out and extract.

## STAINLESS FASTENERS

Another way to get a shiny bolt or nut is to use stainless hardware. And while it is pretty and won't discolor, it simply isn't as strong as most good steel bolts. In fact, a Grade 8 stainless bolt is only about as good as a Grade 2 or 3 SAE steel bolt. The additional problem is the tendency of stainless to gall when the same bright material is used for both the nut and bolt. This ability to readily gall means you need to use anti-seize or Loctite on the threads of any stainless fasteners to prevent metal to metal contact.

Yes, there are some very strong stainless bolts available, but most come from specialty suppliers, not your average aftermarket V-twin shop. The stainless that we see is usually a 300 series alloy. The high strength stainless alloys are of a different make up and actually do corrode! So if you're fond of stainless, use it for non critical applications where big clamping loads aren't required.

You wouldn't use a small carburetor on a 120 cubic inch engine, and in the same way, you don't want to use a cheap bolt for a high-load situation. Understand that not all bolts are created equal and learn to tell the difference between the good ones and the not-so-good ones.

*The two most common ways to ensure the bolt doesn't back out of the hole is with a split-ring lock washer or a "Nylock" type of self-locking nut. Experts prefer the nylon-collar lock nut.*

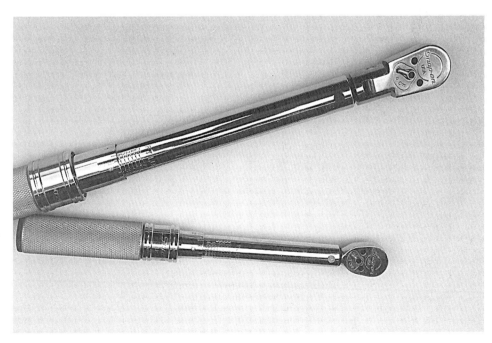

*You can't rely solely on Loctite to keep the bolts in place. A properly torqued nut or bolt actually stretches slightly, which keeps the bolt tight - but you have to get it tight to keep it tight and the best way to do that is with a torque wrench.*

With the upper motor mount in place Rob can mark the frame, and then drill one hole to locate the mount.

The first inner spacer seen here will position the caliper bracket away from the rotor. Next comes the caliper bracket and then the outer axle spacer.

Rob wants the pulley positioned on the hub so the inner edge lines up with the outer edge of the tire – so the belt will clear the tire. Axle spacer should stick out past the outer pulley by 1/16 to 1/8 inch – for a starting point.

With the caliper bracket in place Rob can measure for the final right side axle spacer. With all the spacers in place Rob will tighten the belt to see how it tracks.

Then he pushes the wheel all the way to the left and measures for the right side spacers. Though they can cut spacers in house, an assortment is available from Paul Yaffe.

This is another look at the two spacers and caliper bracket on the right side. The pen points to the outer-most axle spacer.

With the belt tightened and the axle straight in the frame the belt should track in the middle of the pulley when the wheel is rotated in a forward direction.

Rob uses a long straight tube to ensure the tire lines up with the backbone. "My goal is to get the tire in the center and make sure the belt tracks good."

For ride height the boys at Donnie's like about 3-1/2 to 4 inches, "But some of the rigids won't let you get that low," explains Rob.

With the driveline in place it's time to install the tin. The old drive belt placed on the tire will provide about 1/2 inch of clearance.

Before drilling any holes it's a good idea to get the fender positioned on the tire and then stand back for a good look.

119

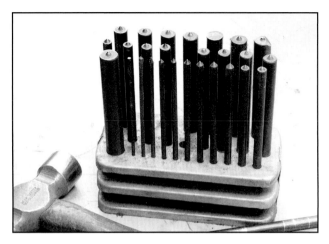

These are transfer punches, available for various hole diameters – a neat way to mark the exact center of a hole.

Because this is a rigid another belt is wrapped on the rear tire and then the fender is set in position.

With the fender in position Rob used the transfer punch to mark the center of the hole. Rob marks and drills these one at a time for accurate placement of the fender.

Rob likes to use small bungs like the one shown to mount the fender. He often uses struts inside or outside the fender so it doesn't need support at the outer end.

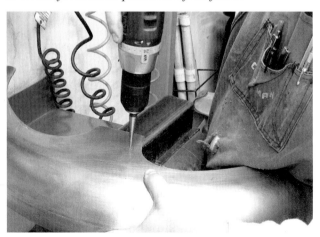

The hole itself is drilled with a step-drill, which cuts a much neater and more accurate hole in sheet metal than a standard fluted drill.

For anyone who wants to use two supports at the end of the fender, a bung can be welded to a piece of tubing or strap as shown.

Once the tank is in the correct position on the top tube, it's time to figure out the dimensions of the T mount for the front of the tank.

Like most calipers, this four piston front caliper comes with mounting bolts and shims to center it over the rotor. "Bolts need to be grade 8" says Rob.

The mitered pipe will be welded to the strap and then welded to the bottom of the top tube. Rubber bushings are the standard "fat bob" bushings.

Here you can see how the shims would be used to move the caliper inside. "You want the split in the caliper centered right over the rotor," explains Rob.

We declare the mock up finished. Now comes a certain amount of welding, followed by painting, chrome plating and final assembly.

# Chapter Eleven

# A Cory Ness Chopper

## A 40 Degree Neck with Zero-Degree Trees

The chopper seen here is being assembled at the Arlen Ness shop in San Leandro, California for Cory Ness. Cory wanted a modern chopper. A bike that he could use to display a number of the many new items in the Arlen Ness catalog.

The project bike starts as a Daytec/Arlen Ness frame (part number 06-806) with 5 inches of top-tube stretch, 4 inches of down-tube stretch and a 40 degree rake, with zero-degree trees. "They handle really nice," explains Jeff, one of the mechanics

*Everyone has their own ideas as to what makes a chopper. While some are raw, Cory and crew decided to build a chopper more deluxe than deprived. Based on a Daytec frame with raised neck, the new bike displays nice lines and that essential chopper silhouette.*

in the shop. "You might not think so but they do"

## WORK BEGINS

The first job is to assemble the front end assembly. Jeff starts with 41mm tubes 31 inches in length. The choice of tube length is a matter of experience, based on the fact that Jeff has already assembled another bike based on the same frame. Assembling the forks starts as Jeff mates each tube with the chrome plated lower leg. First the lower stop is added to the damper rod, then the fork tube is slid down into the lower leg. Next, an Allen bolt with sealing washer is inserted through the bottom of the lower leg to hold the whole thing together.

Now it's time to put in the fork seal, preceded by a the bushing and washer. Jeff uses a home-made seal driver though commercial drivers are available for this job as well. As always, the sealing lip is coated with a light coat of oil before installation. The seal is held in place with a snap ring, the last piece Jeff installs to make a complete fork tube assembly.

At this point the fork tubes are set aside until they're needed farther along in the assembly sequence. For reference, the tubes are 30 inches in length, while the tube and lower legs measure 39 inches fully extended.

The engine for this bike is a polished 97 cubic inch unit from S&S. The frame is one that was used for the new catalog so instead of being bare steel this frame is already painted, with the motor

*Here Jeff inserts the 41mm extended tube into the chrome plated lower leg. The fork seal will be added later.*

*The Allen bolt is what really holds it all together.*

*Here you see the seal, before it is driven into place with a special driver.*

123

*The start: a bare Daytec frame. Note, the pads where the engine and tranny seat have been masked off so there is no paint between engine/tranny and frame.*

*A variety of bolt kits like this motor mount kit make bike assembly much simpler and saves chasing parts.*

*After a test fit the engine is installed. The small bracket being installed at the very front of the engine is a mounting pad for the regulator.*

mounting areas carefully masked off. Before setting the engine in the frame for the first time Jeff and Tim wrap the frame tubes with protective foam.

After the first test fit, Jeff and Tim realize they will have to create a little clearance with the grinder between the rear engine mount and the vertical tube that runs between the engine and transmission.

For the final engine installation they wrap rubber bands around the rear motor mount bolts to hold them up until the motor is dropped in the frame. Once in the frame the rubber bands are removed and the bolts drop right into place. The small bracket that mounts the voltage regulator is installed now, held to the frame with the front engine mounting bolts.

Because this was a display frame the pivot shaft and swingarm are already in place and must be removed. Tim and Jeff (check photos) remove the pivot shaft, set the drive belt in place and re-install the pivot shaft, being careful to tighten the pivot bolts to the correct torque specification (120 to 150 foot pounds).

Next, the five-speed transmission with the polished case is set into the frame. At this point the motor mount and tranny mount bolts are only snug and won't be fully tightened until the inner primary is installed.

The inner and outer primary and related parts all have to be matched to the engine, transmission and frame style. Arlen and Cory have put together a print out that lists all the correct and compatible part numbers. Before installing the inner primary housing the boys install the inner snap ring, the inner primary bearing and the top snap ring. Also the mainshaft seal and the starter shaft seal. As always, a little pre-lube is a good idea for any new bearing.

In order to move the final drive over far enough that the belt clears the tire, a spacer is used between the inner primary and the engine. This 1/2 inch spacer, used with this particular frame, will leave plenty of room for a 180 or 200 series rear tire.

Before the inner primary is set in place a little sealer is smeared around the bolt holes at the rear of the engine and the front of the transmission.

This is to prevent oil seeping past the shank of the bolt and out between the inner primary and the engine or transmission case.

At this point the engine and tranny bolts are only snug. Jeff and Tim install the inner primary and tighten it according to the torque recommendations in the service manual. Once the inner primary bolts are fully tightened the engine and transmission mounting bolts can be tightened. As described elsewhere in this book, some mechanics take the extra step of removing the primary again, after the engine and tranny bolts are tightened. By making sure the inner primary will slide off and on easily, they can be sure the alignment of the engine and transmission is correct.

Of note, this frame does not require the use of a separate mounting plate under the transmission. The holes in the built-in mounting plate are drilled to position the transmission with 1/2 inch of offset, the same dimension used on the engine spacer. You do however, have to use a small extension bracket on the outer right side transmission mounting bolt.

Shock installation is next. This is a task that's much easier because the neck is already strapped down which lifts the ass-end of the frame high in the air to make access to the tranny mounting bolts as easy as possible. For this bike adjustable length Progressive shocks are used.

The starter used here is a 1.6 KW unit from Terry Components. Jeff starts by putting the short coupling on the starter shaft, then bolting the starter in to the right side of the inner primary. The small jackshaft seal was installed earlier. With the starter mounted Jeff adds the jack shaft and then the outer drive coupling, then the drive pinion, and finally the long small-diameter bolt with locking tab that holds the drive gear on the starter shaft.

The primary drive is made up of a stock-style two-row chain and compensator-sprocket assembly with 1/2 inch of offset. The primary drive is essentially stock, except for the extra-plate Kevlar clutch pack from Barnett (A-N #03-124).

Before assembling the primary assembly on the bench Jeff carefully pre-lubes all the compensator

*The pivot shaft had to be removed, and then reinstalled so the belt could be slipped into place.*

*The transmission is a complete 5-speed with polished case from the Arlen Ness catalogue.*

*The primary bearing must be pressed into place in the inner primary. This bearing should be pre-lubed before the inner primary is installed.*

A little sealer applied as shown will keep the primary lube from leaking past the bolt shank.

Jeff and the boys crank the neck down to make tightening of the tranny bolts and installation of the shocks much easier.

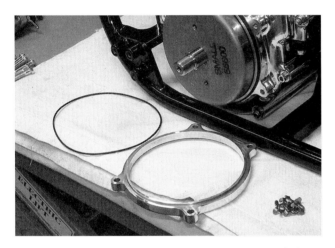

A spacer is used between the inner primary and the engine.

Tranny bolts are tightened last, and then the shocks can be installed.

Now the inner primary can be screwed up against the engine and transmission.

Here you can see the small bracket used between the tranny and the frame's right side mounting tab.

Adjustable length shocks from Progressive are used on this bike, installed with the aid of another bolt kit.

After the starter is installed the jackshaft can be pre-lubed and slipped into place.

The shocks are installed one at a time with a little Loctite on the threads of the bolts.

Next comes the outer coupling (most service manuals have a good blow up of the starter and drive parts).

The Daytec frame kit includes this cover designed to protect the shocks when you ease over a speed bump.

After installing the drive Jeff screws in the long jack-shaft bolt with the small locking-tab washer under the head.

127

*The primary drive for this bike is a standard double row chain with off-set compensator sprocket and Kevlar clutch.*

*The mainshaft nut is left hand thread!*

*The factory manual recommends 5/8 to 7/8 inch of play with the engine cold.*

sprocket parts. Now the primary is installed and the play of the chain is adjusted with the shoe at the bottom of the inner primary.

Jeff uses a small ruler, after the primary is installed, to ensure the chain is "straight" across the outer edge of the inner primary.

### FORK ASSEMBLY

Jeff starts by disassembling the A-N Massive Glide triple tree assembly. Jeff attaches the "cans" to the lower tree, each one is held in place by three screws that thread into the flange on top of each can. Of note, these cans are 18 inches in length and can be cut to a shorter dimension. Next he installs the bottom tapered Timken bearing which was already packed with boat-trailer wheel bearing grease which won't be contaminated by water.

After dropping the upper tapered bearing in place in the neck Jeff and Tim slide the lower triple-tree assembly up into place, and tighten the upper tapered bolt that screws into the stem.

With the triple tree assembly in place Jeff can slide the fork tube assembly up into place. Next he tightens the top nut, then the two cam locks that hold the fork tube into the triple trees, though the new triple trees use a conventional pinch bolt.

### INSTALL REAR WHEEL

Now comes installation of the rear wheel with the brake rotor and drive pulley already attached (the front wheel will come later). The wheel itself is a A-N #25-349 wrapped in a 180/18 Avon tire

Jeff starts by centering the wheel and tire in the swingarm. As he explains the process, "then I see where the belt runs, you can offset the wheel from the centerline but I like to line it up with the top tube so I know it's centered. If the wheel is in the center and the belt is running straight then I measure for spacers, install them and then check it again after I've made the spacers.

The belt is tightened to the factory specs, 3/8 to 1/2 inch of deflection with the owner on the bike and ten pounds of force pushing on the belt, with the built-in Allen-head adjusting screws positioned ahead of the axle on either side. When he's happy with the belt tension and knows the wheel is straight in the frame, Jeff screws another Allen-head set screw down on top of the adjuster screw to lock the adjuster in position.

*After packing the bearings with waterproof grease Jeff drives the bottom bearing down on to the stem.*

*Tube assemblies are next, Jeff installs the top nut first, then the cam-bolt in the lower triple tree.*

*Next, Jeff and Tim install the lower section of the triple tree assembly up into the neck and drop in the upper bearing.*

*Rear wheel installation and adjustment is next. The goal is a belt that runs straight and a tire that's in the center of the frame.*

*Now the top triple tree can be installed and the Allen bolt screwed down into the stem.*

*Once the belt runs true and the wheel is correctly positioned in the frame it's time to measure for axle spacers.*

*After the wheel is correctly positioned and the belt has the right tension, a locking Allen bolt is screwed down on top of the adjuster.*

*The front wheel is installed and then centered between the fork's lower legs. Jeff measures and makes one spacer, installs it and then measures for the other side.*

*The front caliper is a 4 piston caliper that comes with it's own bracket and shims to center it over the rotor.*

## INSTALL FRONT WHEEL AND BRAKE

The installation procedure followed for the front wheel is similar to that followed for the rear, if only a bit simpler due to the missing belt. The wheel itself is a "Fat 40" A-N #25-310 with a 90-21 Avon front tire. Jeff hangs the wheel on the axle, then centers it between the lower legs, makes a spacer for one side, installs that spacer, then measures and cuts the spacer for the other side. This front wheel uses the 2000 and later sealed wheel bearing.

Like all calipers with opposing pistons, the four-piston Arlen Ness caliper that Jeff installs must be mounted so it is centered over the rotor, to ensure that the caliper housing can't rub on the rotor and that the pistons on either side of the caliper move out of their bores the same amount on application. As a rule of thumb Jeff likes to have 1/2 inch between the inside of the caliper mounting bracket and the surface of the rotor. Once he has the caliper mounted he can do a final check of the position and fine tune the position of the caliper with the caliper-to-bracket spacers provided in the kit.

At this point Cory and Jeff install the new bars into new riser bushings. Jeff wraps a piece of shim stock around the rubber grommet for the risers so the bars will be grounded.

## SHEET METAL STAGE ONE

Installing the sheet metal is done in two stages. After Cory helped with the installation of the handle bars, he and the crew spend time trying different fenders on the bike.

The final choice for a rear fender is a Legacy, chosen from the many shapes available from the Arlen Ness catalog. The fender fits reasonably well, though in order to create a match between the radius of the fender and the edge of the wheel rim Tim and Jeff have to loosen the belt tension and slide the wheel forward slightly. This means that before the bike is final-assembled they will have to alter the mounting bracket for the fender so it can be positioned farther back on the frame. With softtail type frames it's also important to make sure there's enough clearance on the left side between the fender and the swingarm when the suspension is fully compressed. For a front fender they try a

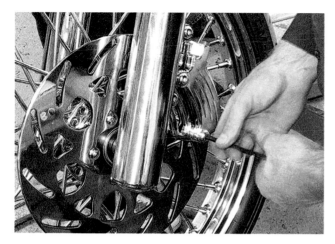

As a general rule Jeff likes to have 1/2 inch between the inside of the bracket and the outside of the rotor, that positions the caliper correctly over the rotor.

The front fender comes from stock too, a cafe' design that Cory checks for fit.

Cory and Tim install the bars with their integral risers. Bars need to be grounded if the turn signals mount to the bars and do not have a ground wire.

This is the rear caliper and bracket that are used on this bike. The caliper bracket was installed with the rear wheel, but the caliper was not.....

At Arlen and Cory's shop they have the luxury of trying out a number of fenders before deciding which one they like the best.

....so when the caliper was finally installed on the bracket it turns out that the rotor is too far in, or the caliper too far out.

few and end up with a trim fender, A-N#07-820, positioned over the front wheel.

## INSTALLATION OF THE REAR CALIPER

Installation of the rear caliper comes next, and illustrates the little things that can go wrong during the construction of a motorcycle, even by a crew that does this all the time. With the bracket in place Tim tries to install the caliper only to discover that the rotor is positioned too far in, a situation that can't be easily rectified by simply placing shims between the bracket and the caliper. Instead the crew will have to either place a spacer between the rotor and the wheel, or use a smaller spacer between hub and caliper bracket - and then a longer spacer between the caliper bracket and the frame.

## MORE SHEET METAL

Once the rear fender is attached it's time to choose a gas tank.

The tank that the boys choose, a five inch stretch model from Independent, (A-N#07-76), is formed in steel. Though there are mounting bungs in the bottom of the tank, there are no brackets on the frame. Jeff uses the mounting kit that comes with the tank, and an additional piece of steel, to fabricate the tank-mounting brackets. The mounting kit includes two brackets with the commonly used "fat bob" rub-

*The shape and exact position of the tank is critical to the look of the bike. It pays to take time before you start making brackets.*

*The bottom of the tank shows the bracket that Jeff made from the supplied kit and an extra piece of strap.*

ber bushings. Though the idea of mounting a tank seems pretty simple, you have to remember that when filled with gas, the tank is fairly heavy and that the brackets are subject to considerable vibration. Jeff gets the tank up off the top bar with rubber padding that is normally used as a cushion under a battery. The mounting brackets themselves are fabricated carefully in a series of steps best illustrated in the accompanying photos.

*The bottom of the tank after the fabrication of the mounting brackets.*

What's left now is the choosing of a seat, and then the mock up is finished. Though the seat for this bike will be a custom piece, based on a fabricated seat pan, those of us working at home might want to have the finished seat in hand before deciding on the final position of the gas tank(s).

Most mock ups require the complete disassembly of the bike so the frame and all the rest can be painted. Because this frame is painted it's possible to simply pull off the sheet metal for painting, find the best way to change the position of the rear caliper, and then finish the final assembly of the motorcycle.

*The 'finished' bike complete with radius outer primary*

## Chapter Twelve

# An American Thunder Chopper

## A Springer Fork and 250 Rear Tire

The sequence shown here documents the mock up of a wide tire, right side drive, Rolling Thunder chassis at the American Thunder shop in Prior Lake, Minnesota. Even for a shop that assembles bikes full time, a mock up is good idea to ensure all the holes line up and that everything fits.

Called a "250 Chopper kit," the frame is a Rolling Thunder design wide enough to accept a 250 rear tire and a right-side-drive transmission

*The bike assembled for this sequence is based on the American Thunder 250 chopper kit seen here. Though there is no running gear, the kit is otherwise pretty complete and includes frame, suspension, fork, sheet metal, wheels and axles.*

from Baker. This particular soft-tail type frame is extended two inches out and six inches up and has the neck angle set at 46 degrees. Up front the boys will install a Rolling Thunder springer. This springer is designed to work on this frame so Ken and Neil know that both the ride height and trail will be correct. A nice feature, this frame and fork combination use internal fork stops. The tires measure 250/40/18 for the rear and 90/21 up front, both are from Avon.

## THE ASSEMBLY STARTS

Ken Mlsna starts the assembly by strapping the bare frame in place on the work bench. Then he starts on what he calls frame preparation, "the clearance is pretty tight where the swingarm pivot bolt goes through the frame," explains Ken, "so you may have to clean out the paint or the powder coat. And I like to run a tap into all the holes to clean the paint out of the threads."

The outer races for the neck bearings are installed next. Ken hammers each race in place, using the correct bearing driver, until he can feel the race is seated. To install the fork he first removes the top tree and then the neck retaining nut. The bearings are packed in a small packer with Bel Ray waterproof grease.

Ken sets the top bearing and dust shield in place in the neck. Then, with the lower bearing in place on the stem, he slides the fork assembly up into place and screws the top retaining nut in place. About adjusting the stem nut Ken pretty much follows the recommendation in a factory service manual and adds, "There shouldn't be any play in the bearings. With a standard front end and the fork pointed straight ahead on the hoist (with the front wheel in place) you want it to flop over after you tap it a couple of times. It's harder to adjust the bearings with the long front ends."

The springer from Rolling Thunder comes in a wide glide configuration, and holes of the correct spacing and size for standard risers, "So

*The project starts with the already primered frame strapped to the bench.*

*The swingarm pivot bearings have to be driven into the swingarm before it is installed.*

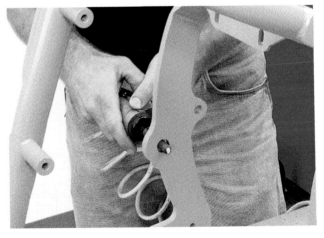

*There is always a build up of paint or powder paint on the inside of the holes like this one. When clearance is tight the hole needs to be cleaned up.*

135

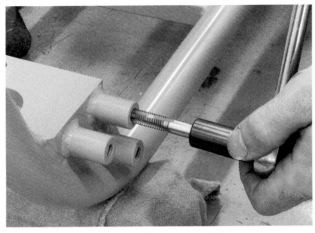

Running a tap into all the threaded holes ia a very necessary part of prepping the frame, better to find the dirty threads now.

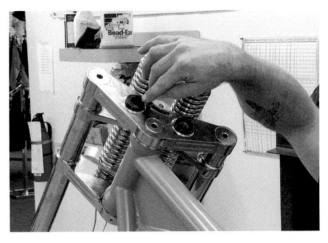

This upper tree accepts standard bushings and has standard spacing, not all of them do.

A driver is used to install the inner race for the upper and lower steering head bearings.

The handlebars used here have integral risers and are held in place by bolts that come in from the bottom.

Now the fork can be installed and the upper stem nut adjusted.

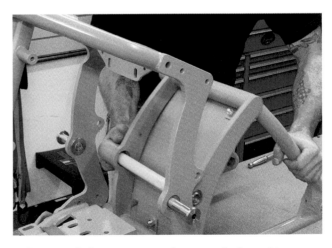

The pivot bolts screw into the cross shaft, a thin washer is used between the swingarm and the inside of the frame.

your options on handle bars are unlimited," adds Ken.

The bars, with integral risers, are called "chubby pull-backs" and come with the frame kit. Installation is pretty straightforward though Ken does take the tap to the female threads on the bottom of the risers, and he uses paraffin on the chrome-plated bolts that screw into the risers from the bottom.

## INSTALL SWINGARM AND SHEET METAL

Ken starts the installation of the swingarm by coating the bolts with anti-seize, the frame has already been "clearanced" for the bolts. Though this is only the mock up, for final assembly these bolts are torqued to 120 foot pounds. Shock bolts get coated with anti-seize too. Ken leaves the left side shock out so we can more easily mount the tranny and show correct alignment procedures for the engine and transmission. Note: Normally the drive belt is installed before the swingarm. Due to confusion about how far we were taking this mock up the belt was not installed prior to the swingarm which meant the swingarm had to be pulled out again later so the belt could be installed.

Tank installation is next. With more conventional frames where the tank sits down lower than this one, "you might want to install the engine first and then the tanks" advises Ken. The small rubber grommets use to mount the tank are the same ones used for mounting fat bob tanks. After running a tap up into the female fasteners on the bottom of the tank Ken sets it in place and screws in four bolts.

Next on the agenda is installation of the forward controls, which come with the kit. With the forward controls in place it's time to install the kick stand bracket which bolts to the left side control. On final assembly "you definitely want to use blue Loctite on these bolts," advises Ken.

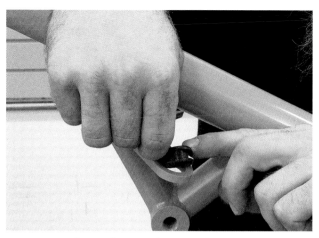

*Mounting the tank is made easier because the brackets are already welded to the frame. Ken installs the standard fat bob bushings.*

*As you can see the tank is well supported and held in place by four bolts that screw in from underneath.*

*The forward controls are part of the kit, as is the kickstand. For final assembly all the bolts will get a shot of Loctite.*

137

The front wheel is installed and spaced to be in the center of the fork.

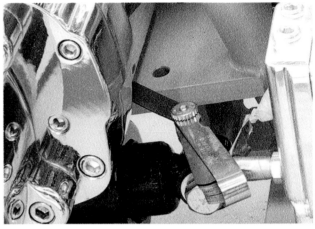

After the engine bolts are tightened the tranny must be checked for clearance between the mounting point and the frame. Excess clearance can be shimmed.

After the engine is set into the frame Ken drops the engine mounting bolts down into place.

In this case Ken had to use a spacer between the hub and the inside of the pulley.

The inner primary is tightened to spec before the engine and transmission are final-tightened.

The ruler should just slide down inside the pulley, the idea is to have the pulley over far enough that the belt clears the tire.

## INSTALL THE WHEELS

Before installing the front wheel Ken likes to coat the axle with a little grease or anti-seize. The wheels used here are 60 spoke assemblies from Road Wings. For the mock up Ken just finds some spacers that are close to being the right dimension and uses those. As a note, if Ken were to use a mechanical speedometer on this bike he would first have to machine a small notch in the left side of the hub to accept the pin on the speedometer drive mechanism. The front axle is from Rolling Thunder, and the specialized threaded end is torqued per the specifications from RT.

Spacing and aligning the rear wheel is something that each kit builder will have to do for themselves. "We don't generally send rear wheel spacers with the kits because we don't know what people are running for brakes, and that affects the spacing," explains Ken. "If we know, then we can ship them the correct spacers." At his point Ken simply slides the rear wheel into the frame without any spacers for a quick look at how it lines up.

Before setting the engine in the frame (with help from Troy) Ken tapes the two rear engine mounting bolts up and out of the way so once the engine is in the frame all he has to do is pull the tape and drop them into the holes in the frame. The transmission is a Baker five speed, RSD, that mounts directly into the frame without a separate mounting plate.

As has been explained before, the engine and transmission bolts are left loose until the inner primary is installed and torqued to specifications. Then the engine bolts are tightened, and the transmission is checked to see if shims are needed between the housing and the frame. Finally, the transmission-to-frame nuts can be tightened with shims in place as needed. As a final check the inner primary should go on and off easily after the transmission bolts are torqued to factory specifications.

*Here Ken uses the simple alignment tool described in all the factory manuals to get the wheel straight in the frame.*

*A snap gauge can be set down into the space between wheel and frame....*

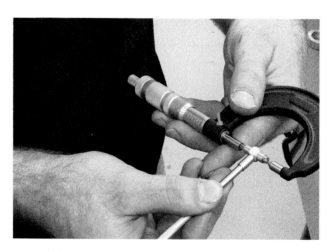

*...and then pulled out and measured. An easy way to measure for the axle spacers.*

At this point Ken pulls the swingarm out and installs the belt, then he puts a pulley on the rear wheel, with a spacer, and reinstalls the wheel. "We usually install a 65 tooth pulley," explains Ken. "The center to center distance for the transmission and the rear pulley is the same as on a factory bike, so the belt we use is the same 130 tooth belt as a stock Softail with a 65 tooth sprocket.

For rear wheel align-

*Axle spacers like these are cut on an as-needed basis.*

*The idea is to get the belt to run straight, and not crowd up against either side of the pulley. Obviously you need clearance between the pulley and tire, and pulley and frame.*

ment, Ken likes to start by getting the rear wheel roughly in position, centered front to back and straight in the frame. Then with tension on the belt he uses a snap gauge to determine width of the spacers. "We make spacers from PVC pipe for the roller chassis we take to the shows," explains Ken. To adjust the belt, Ken uses the factory approved spring-loaded gauge. With the gauge putting ten pounds of pressure on the belt it should deflect 3/8 to 1/2 inch (with the rider on the bike). "If everything is lined up right," says Ken, "you should be able to rotate the wheel in a forward direction and have the belt stay in the center of the wheel pulley and not crowd up against the outer edge of the drive pulley.

There are a few more pieces to install before the whole thing comes apart again. The oil tank and brackets are part of the frame kit. What isn't part of the frame kit is the fiberglass seat pad, though it's available as an option. With the smooth seat pan, "You have to use a Odyssey battery," says Ken, "because it has the lowest profile." If you want to run a regular 16 size battery you need a seat pan with a bump-out for the battery.

What's left is the installation of the very wide rear fender and probably the brakes (not shown). The idea is to ensure that all the parts fit, that all the holes line up, that none of the threads are stripped – before the parts are sent out for final paint and polishing.

*The oil tank is part of the kit, and is installed with rubber mounted brackets that allow for some adjustment of tank-to-frame fit.*

*The kit concept makes bike building much simpler.. A mock up is still a good idea, but things like the fit of the sheet metal and the length of the fork have all been worked out.*

## BUILD THE ULTIMATE V-TWIN MOTORCYCLE

10 chapters include:
- Build what's right for you
- Start with the right frame
- Use the best fork & suspension
- How much motor is enough
- Registration and insurance
- Paint or powder coat
- Sheet metal
- Assembly photo sequences

Ten Chapters     144 Pages

Publisher Tim Remus sought out the top custom bike builders to share their expertise with you. Hundreds of photos illustrate the extensive text. This is a revised edition with updated information and new products. If you're dreaming of the Ultimate V-Twin this is the place to start.

$19.95

## BUILD THE ULTIMATE V-TWIN CHASSIS

Ten chapters with 250+ photos.
- Frame buyers guide
- Which fork to buy
- Installing the driveline
- Sheet metal choices
- Powder coat or paint
- Mount a super wide rear tire
- How to pick the best brakes
- Understand motorcycle wiring

Ten Chapters     144 Pages

The foundation of any custom or scratch-built motorcycle is the frame. The look, ride and handling are all determined by the chassis. This book is part Buyer's Guide and part Assembly Manual. Shop Tours of Arlen Ness and M-C Specialties. Newly revised.

$19.95

## AMERICAN V-TWIN ENGINE

Everything you need to build or buy the right V-twin motor for your dream ride. Informative text illustrated with more than 300 photos.

- TC History
- TC Development
- TC 88-B
- TC Troubles
- TC Hop Up
- TC Cam & Big-Bore install
- Evo Planning
- Evo Carbs

- Evo Cams
- Evo Head & Porting
- Evo Combinations
- Evo Big Block Engines
- Evo Cam Install & Engine Assembly

A large Sources section

Fourteen Chapters     160 Pages

$21.95

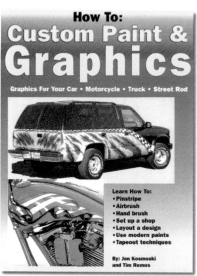

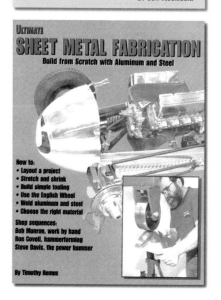

# Sources

American Thunder
16760 Toronto Avenue
Prior Lake, MN 55372
952 226 1180

Accurate Engineering
128 Southgate Road
Dolhan, AL 36301
334 702 1993

Aeroquip (Eaton Aeroquip)
Performance Products
3000 Strayer Rd
Maumee, OH 43537
419 891 5100
www.aeroquip.com

Arlen Ness Inc.
16520 E 14th St.
San Leandro, CA 94578
510 276 3395

Baker Transmissions
9804 E Saginaw
Haslett, MI 48840
517 339 3835

Buchanan's Spoke and Rim
805 W Eighth St.
Azusa, CA 91702
626 969 4655

Chrome Specialties Inc.
4200 Diplomacy Road
Fort Worth, TX 76155
800 277 8685 to find a dealer.
www.chromespecialties.com

Custom Chrome
800 359 5700
www.customchrome.com

Custom Cycle Creations
6108 Avenida Encinas Suite A
Carlsbad, CA 92009
760 930 0172
www.customcyclecreations.com

Cyril Huze Customs
3500 NW Boca Raton Boulevard, #809
Boca Raton, FL 33431
561 347 1616
www.cyrilhuze.com

Delano Harley-Davidson
4354 US Hwy 12 SE
Delano, MN 55328
763 479-2530

Donnie Smith Custom Cycles
10594 Raddison Road NE
Blaine, MN 55449
612 786 6002

Kokesh MC parts
8302 NE Hwy 65
Spring Lake Park, MN 55432
763 786 9050

Knucklehead Power USA
5715 Pinkney Avenue
Sarasota, FL 34233
941 921 4762

Independent Gas Tank Company
480 633 6700
FAX:  480 855 9647
www.independentgastank.com

Johnson, Kendall
Killer Klown wheels and killer V-twins
8720 Dennis Road
Germanton, NC 27019
336 595 9339

Jim's Manufacturing
531 Dawson Drive  Unit F
Camarillo, CA 93012
805 482 6913

Lee's Speed Shop
1422 3rd Avenue
Shakopee MN 55379
952 233 2782

Letourneau, Neal
308 Lion Lane
Shoreview, MN 55126
651 483 6958

Odyssey Batteries
West Coast Battery
PO Box 1177
Windsor, CA 95492
707 838 7741
www.odysseybatteries.com

Panzer
PO Box 425
Canon City, CO 81215
719 269 7267
www.panhead.com

Pat Kennedy's MC
PO Box 670
Tombstone, AZ 85638
520 432 1330 FAX 520 432 1317
www.kennedyschopper.com

Performance Machine
6892 Marlin Circle
LaPalma, CA 90623
714 523 3000

Rad Paint
7129 20th Avenue North
Centerville,  MN 55038
651 426 7161

Rivera Engineering
12532 Lambert Road
Whittier, CA 90606
562 907 2600

Rolling Thunder
1810 Ford Boulevard
Chateauguay, QC J6J 4Z2 CAN
450 699 7045
www.rollingthunderframes.com

TP Engineering
5 Frances J. Clarke Circle
Bethel, CT 06801
203 744 4960

Tuff Cycle
1375 Route 43
Aurora, OH 44202
330 995 0775

S&S Cycle
Box 215 - RT 2, County G
Viola, WI 54664
608 627 1497

STD, High Performqnce Components
PO Box 3583
Chatsworth, CA 91313-3583
818 998 8226

Zipper's Cycle Inc.
6655A Amberton Drive
Elkridge, MD 21075
410 579 2100